T0090358

GOlf

the
Game Of Lessening Failures

BY

BOB
GLANVILLE

Order this book online at www.trafford.com
or email orders@trafford.com

Most Trafford titles are also available at major online book retailers.

Printed in the United States of America.

ISBN: 978-1-4269-4392-8 (sc)
ISBN: 978-1-4269-4393-5 (hc)
ISBN: 978-1-4269-4394-2 (e)

Library of Congress Control Number: 2010914173

Trafford rev. 02/01/2011

Trafford
PUBLISHING   www.trafford.com

North America & international
toll-free: 1 888 232 4444 (USA & Canada)
phone: 250 383 6864 ♦ fax: 812 355 4082

INTRODUCTION

So why did I write a book? Well, besides having a lot of proven facts plus some useless but humorous data along with a few personal stories to share, I have a different theory about golf that maybe, just maybe, will help many new and old golfers with their game. It's for those golfers who keep trying every gimmick and trick offered, in short doses by fellow players and such, but yet not LESSENING the number of FAILURES they experience on the golf course as they should but could with correct information. This book provides lots of information about the basic attributes that go into golf. But also, it incorporates my aspect of how to improve your game beyond the physical aspects by suggesting some different ideas to the very important, but usually overlooked or misguided mental aspect of the game.

A THEORY, I propose, is a supposition proposed as true with some evidence to back it up but very little fact to corroborate its actually being true. For example: Darwin's Theory of Evolution is supported by some evidence but not much fact. Darwin himself says that it is a <u>Theory</u>, his Theory as to what has happened and is happening. It has little evidence supporting it, but is accepted as truth by many people with or without the facts to back it up.

What does this have to do with golf? Well I have a <u>Theory</u> about the game, which has several facts to corroborate its authenticity, such as: (a) golf is a game of <u>swinging</u> a club, not <u>hitting</u> a ball (Lee Travino proved that you can use most anything swingable to hit a ball correctly. So, is it the correct and consistent <u>swinging</u> of an object or is it the <u>hitting</u> that makes the ball go in the right direction?); (b) a golf swing is very individual and "one swing does <u>not</u> fit all" and it changes constantly which causes the player to have to be able to mentally and physically adapt to the changing environment; (c) the game IS a mix of physical ability and mental control (more games are won and lost do to the latter rather than the physical aspect); (d) the more you know about the game and it's rules the more you will like it and the better you will probably play; (e) the more you play and practice the better you get; (f) the equipment you use does make a difference. (A good set of fitted clubs will play much better than a tree branch Lee Travino was said to have used once to win a bet. By the way, it was also said that he cut that branch and shaped it and practiced with it awhile before placing it at the most convenient location to be used at just the right time.)

As with any theory presented for scrutiny it should have facts and figures, technical data and a lot of common sense mixed in to prove its validity. I hope to have provided all these in this book and after reading it, I hope it has enhanced your knowledge as to the Game's history and language, but more than those, provided you with information on how you can accomplish "Lessening your Failures" on the golf course. Some parts get pretty technical, which may be boring to a "Real Golfer" (definition to be explained later) but if you stick with it, you will learn things that just may turn your game around.

It has been said: Learn from your Failures" which is advice we all can use since we do have a tendency to fail. But, you can either learn; how to fail the same way in bigger and better ways, or how to _not_ repeat the same failures, but rather try anew and possibly, or not, to fail differently. Now before you get too upset about that statement and think I am a defeatist, let me remind you that we are talking about the game of golf not life. The golf related failures are fixable even though numerable.

We must change and continually change what we do and how we do it because of the nature of the game, how it is played and the environment which it is played. We and our swing will evolve as we; get older, stronger (or weaker), practice and play. Hence we will fail. Trying something new sets us up to fail again and even again and again.

But, the result is: we can get better! Eliminating the failures one at a time (sometimes a single failure causes many others). Failing, is the part of the game because of its many facetted elements. But, a lot of the problems encountered on the golf course can be combated mentally rather than physically. My hope is that this book provides the enlightenment as to how to improve your mental game as well as your physical one.

Over the past 20+ years of teaching and helping others to play better, I have gathered a lot of information that I believe is worth sharing. A great portion of the following information I heard from friends, from other players, and from playing/teaching professionals. For the most part I did a lot of research in: magazines such as GOLF, Golf Digest, Golf Magazine, Senior Golf, and Golf Tips; club repair books; and all the books on golf in the public library I could find. I condensed and stored it in my computer to keep track of it for assembly it into some kind of working order for instructional use at a later date. This book is the assemblage of that data collection as well as experiences, observations, opinions, and training of my own. I am just another golfer who loves all aspects of the game, who has achieved a good amount of success in playing and teaching and who wants to help others to accomplish the same.

I have added personal ideas and thoughts about what golf is and how it should be taught and played. I included information that could be beneficial to a wide range of readers, golfers and non golfers, and tried not to be too boring about it. There are parts of this book that will appeal to some more than others, but I am hopeful that all would at least read it through. By doing so, I expect the reader to become a golfer or be a better golfer. I do believe that it is beneficial for that purpose. If the readers find it amusing and enlightening as well as helpful then I accomplished what I intended. I would like people to understand the game better and learn some of the technicalities and terms of the game as well as understanding what their role in the game is, for then, maybe, it could be a beginning of playing better. Moreover, I wanted this book and the game of golf to be an enjoyable experience for everyone. The first half is an easy humorous read while the second half does get more serious but if you're serious about getting better at golf, read on.

For the non-golfers who read this and would possible want to start playing golf, I do stress instruction and continued lessons with practice but, these are not necessary to have fun and enjoy the game only to get better at it. Once bitten by the Golf bug, instruction and practice is the best way to learn to play better while having more fun. Without these elements or one without the other is futile and can lead to frustration, anger and the loss of heart to play this wonderful game.

Overall, this book is about the game of golf, where it came from, what the equipment is, the terms used and some instructional hints to help with personal accomplishments. There are many quotes and copied articles contain within. I tried to give credit to the original writers or to the origin of the quotes, but over the years it has become too difficult to remember who said what and when. Some of the content may not have been credited to the correct author or to an author at all, for that I apologize and hope that I have not done an injustice to them. Some quotes were sent to me via email so the author is unknown. These will be identified with a "www. com"

My thanks to my beloved wife of 17 years, Jacquie now deceased, who through her wondrous patience, love and understanding has allowed me to complete this book and more importantly to continue to use this information on the golf course many days that could have been suited for other worthwhile "at-home" activities. To Chuck Glanville, my Dad, who taught my brother and me how to play golf when I was 12 year's old. Most important, thanks to my Lord Jesus Christ for my faith, health, physical and mental abilities I've needed for the past 60 years to play courses here in the U.S. and overseas. Also, for the talents that He has provided me, to not only to play at the professional level, but to teach at that level so others may be able to play and play better no matter their skill level.

MORE ABOUT THE AUTHOR

Robert L Glanville was born in Oklahoma in 1938. During the WWII years the family moved to Fresno, California, where he and his older brother Jim, would go to the local Country Club and watch the golfers and even possibly to caddie. Bob, being only slightly bigger than the golf bags at that age, had a tough time lifting one, let alone carrying it. One day two gentlemen asked for him to caddie and to carry both bags for them, he accepted. After barely surviving the day, with the help of his bother Jim, he decided that part of golf was not for him.

Eventually the family moved to El Segundo, California. It was there that his step-father Chuck began teaching his mother, himself and brother how to play golf. Chuck first taught Jim and Bob how to caddie correctly, which they did for the first year. Jim got his first set of clubs and began playing soon after. Meanwhile, Bob was still a little too small so it wasn't until the next year that he got a set of clubs too, and the family foursome was set. So at the age of about 12, Bob saw his second golf course and held his first golf club. Trying to hit his first golf ball didn't go very well.

The now "Glanville Foursome" would get up at 5:00 am and drive to Long Beach to play. On many occasions they would get on the first tee at dawn with a fog so thick you could not see the end of the tee box. On those foggy days Bob's golf shoes would be big rubber galoshes, the kind that had metal buckles from mid foot to mid shin. They kept your feet dry but with no spikes on them. At times it was somewhat like playing on ice with rubber soles or better yet, ski boots.

After moving from El Segundo, they also moved away from golf for several years. It was after graduating High School joining the Air Force and getting married did the spark of golf once again ignite. Being stationed

Lowry Air Force Base in Denver, Colorado Bob began playing Wellshire Golf Course and from there played all over the U.S., Japan, Korea, South Vietnam, and Thailand.

Ending up in Hanford, California in the 1980's, is when he became serious about the game and began to take his handicap from a 12 to a +1, through lessons, several seminars, and lots of practice on his way to the Country Club Championship in 1989. He learned more about his swing as he was asked to teach others and help with theirs. All benefited, their handicaps went down as did Bob's and he began to collect, store and assemble data about the golf swing (the physical and mental aspects), dynamics of the game, technologies and technical terms.

While still in Hanford and after losing his wife Patricia to cancer in 1990 he launched a Professional Golf career by joining the Seniors Players Tour, based in Florida, so he could qualify for the Senior PGA events. In 1991 he went to Austin, Texas to attend Golfsmith's week long golf club repair and fitting school. When not playing in tour events, Bob would work at a driving range in Longmont, Colorado, providing golf lessons, building custom fitted golf club sets and performing every kind of golf club repairs.

In 1991 he met Jacquelyn Korinek. In 1993 they were married. Although it was the end of his touring Professional Playing Career other opportunities in the field of golf opened up. Bob still teaches golf. He has taught and worked with the International Students organization at Denver University and still gives private playing lessons when he can. He works for Cherry Creek Country Club in Denver as their Professional Golf Club Repairman taking care of all golf club repairs. Bob is also a Technical Representative for Wilson Staff Golf in Colorado providing Wilson Staff golf equipment for promotional demonstrations. He resides in Centennial, Colorado.

TABLE OF CONTENTS

A SHORT
STORY ABOUT GOLF

Go to the golf course
Hit the Ball
Find the ball
Repeat until the ball is in the hole
Have fun
The end

> Chuck Hogan
> Pro golf coach

Always remember:

"The game of golf is swinging
a golf club, not hitting a ball."

> Bob Glanville - Author

WORDS OF WISDOM
FROM THE WWW INTERNET

"The game of golf is 90% mental and 10% mental."

"Golf can be best described as an endless series of tragedies obscured by the occasional miracle."

" If you find yourself pleased that you locate more balls in the rough than you actually have lost, your focus is totally wrong and your personality might not be right for golf...it is also just a matter of time before the IRS investigates your business."

"Golf is harder than baseball. In golf, you have to play your foul balls."

"In baseball you hit your home run over the right-field fence, the left field fence, the center-field fence. Nobody cares. In golf everything has got to be over second base" Hen Harrelson

"I usually play in the low to mid 80s. If it gets any hotter than that, I won't play."

" Don't buy a putter until you've had a chance to throw it."

" A ball you can see in the rough from 50 yards away is not yours."

" Golfers who claim they don't cheat, also lie."

"The less skilled the player, the more likely he is to share his ideas about the golf swing"

" Never try to keep more than 300 separate thoughts in your mind during your swing."

"It's surprisingly easy to hole a 50-foot putt when you lie 10."

" If there is a ball in the fringe and a ball in the bunker, your ball is the one in the bunker. If both balls are in the bunker, yours is the one in the footprint."

"If you find you do not mind playing golf in the rain, the snow, even during a lightning storm, here's a valuable tip: your life is in trouble."

CHAPTER I

"In the Beginning"

THE GAME OF GOLF

According to the well known author and spinner of adventurous tales, Mark Twain, the game of golf is *"A good walk spoiled."* Winston Churchill: *"Golf is like chasing a quinine pill around a cow pasture."* On the other hand, the game of golf, according to Senior PGA touring professional Chi Chi Rodriguez, is *"The most fun you can have without taking your clothes off."*

All golfers and even non-golfers have their own opinion about the game. Sometimes it seems like it is the worst experience you can have but on other occasions it is the most elating experience unmatched by any other, but only a golfer would know what I mean. *"Golf is not a game, it's bondage. It was obviously devised by a man torn by guilt, eager to atone for his sins."* Anon

If nothing else, it is a game that allows an individual to enjoy nature, other people, and a sense of accomplishment. It is a game that has no limit to the amount of success one can achieve, a game that cannot be beaten but has recorded feats, as goals to obtain or exceed. Yet it is a game that has guidelines and boundaries that are in reach of every player. *"Achieving a certain level of success in golf is only important if you can finally enjoy the level you've reached after you've reached it."* Anon

I have never met a person on a golf course or who has ever played the game, for that matter, who has ever began a game of golf with the idea of playing worst or even as good as they played before. We all believe that we

1

have the capability of playing better each time we tee it up. That is why I named this book: GOLF the *Game Of Lessening Failures*. Don't we strive to play it better than ever before and better than anyone else? Don't we strive to make less mistakes than before by learning from our failures and correcting them?

Golf does requires some physical skills, a lot of practice (to be good at it), and a colossal amount of mental discipline (concentration) if a person really wants to play well. It is also a game that can be enjoyed by those that possess none of the above, no matter the score, no matter the number of mistakes made or the number of great, unforgettable shots. It is a game to be played for pure enjoyment but then that depends on the player's attitude and temperament. It is a game that can bring out the best and/or the worst in people because of the humbling effect it has. But, that is the nature of the game and probably the one main reason golfers keep coming back to play for they just refuse to be humbled by a "stupid kids game" knowing that they can play better.

" Golf is not a life or death situation, it's much more important than that!!" My sentiments exactly but I don't know who the original author was.

As in many other games, golf has its own terminology that is special and unique to the sport. You can *shoot eagles, buzzards and birdies*. As to my game, eagles and birdies are becoming endangered species! *"Bogies"* is a term used by the military to represent enemy elements and so they can be the same in golf too. They can come in single, double or even triple amounts and you're all alone to fight them with just a few *sticks* you carry in a bag. *Least* is best, and being *under* is better and pays more than being *over*. *Par* is what we are talking about but who wants to be just average? We want to be less than that, right? It's a sickness you know, incurable.

A *lie* could be a good thing (a contradiction in terms?) and can be pleasing or it could be bad and cause penalties. It could be a blessing or a sin. *Good lies* are often found in the *fairway* which is sometimes not "fair" at all. *Bad lies* are often found in tall grass, bushes or next to trees in an area called the *rough* because that is what it is when you try to get out of it with just a stick. *Bad lies* can also be found on the score card where a 4 is written in place of a 6 and in the fairway where the ball has come to rest in a *divot* that had to be made by someone mentally resembling a 500 pound gorilla. Even the golf clubs have *lies* built right into them. There are even *buried lies* but we won't go there! (There is a book out called "Golf's Sacred Journey - Seven Days at the Links of Utopia" written by David L. Cook, PhD., with a forward by Tom Lehman, that has a great section on "buried lies". I strongly recommend reading this book).

> *" Golf! You hit down to make the ball go up. You swing left and the ball goes right. The lowest score wins. And on top of that, the winner buys the drinks."* www.com

Even some of the names assigned to the equipment are unique and interesting. *Brassies, spoons, irons, woods,* and *niblicks* are used to put a *gutty* into a *cup*. You always start in a *tee box* with an *address*. Your *clubs* are carried by a *caddie* in a *golf bag* while riding or pulling a *cart*. You hit to a *green* or at a *pin* or *stick* and try to *putt* (not put but putt) the ball into a hole.

> *A little girl was at her first golf lesson when she asked an interesting question; is the word spelled P-U-T or P-U-T-T?" "P-U-T-T is correct,"* the instructor replied. *"PUT means to place a thing where you want it. PUTT means merely a vain attempt to do the same thing."* www.com

You yell "fore" at other players that may be in the way of an errant *shot* instead of *"look-out"* or *"duck"* to keep golf from becoming a contact sport. This single word could possibly be the first of several more off color four-letter words exchanged between golfers. A *left hook* is a misdirected shot to the immediate left not a punch thrown by someone, unless the exchange of four-letter words do make the game into a contact sport, which then could incorporate several meaningful left hooks.

A *sand trap* is not a trap at all (although they do *snare* a lot of golf balls) but deemed to be a *hazard* or a *bunker* (another contradiction in terms?). Isn't a *hazard* a dangerous thing? Isn't a *bunker* considered a safe haven? A *sand trap* could be defined as: "a deep depression filled with sand or tall grass found next to the fairway or green where you find golfers in deep depression." A *hazard* is normally made up of water or sand but not necessarily a danger or peril to the golfer. Unless it is filled with meat eaters or contains poisonous reptiles or is the single cause of a severe loss of cash, which in that case it is at least a peril to the contents of a player's wallet.

An *amateur golfer* is one who plays golf for pleasure. A *golf analyst* is a psychiatric specialist who treats individuals suffering from the delusion that playing golf is a form of pleasure.

At the very least, golf is a game that encourages the habit of honesty because the game is not worth playing if you set out to cheat. If you are so minded, it is ridiculously easy to cheat. Hence *"most golfers develop a deep respect for the rules and a pride in observing them in every particular because they can recognize achievement when scope and boundaries are established. Otherwise, the game has no competitiveness, no since of pride, and becomes meaningless."* Anon.

"I want to get to the day when everything will fall into place; where everything makes sense, when every swing is with confidence, and every shot is exactly what I want. I know it can be done. I've been close enough to smell it a few times, but I'd like to touch it, to feel it. I know it's been touched. Hogan touched it. Byron touched it. I want to touch it. Then, I think I'd be satisfied. Then, and only then, I think I could walk away from the game truly satisfied." Tom Watson[1]

I once overheard a player talking to his partner while playing in a team competition, in which they were not doing very well as a team: " *I know that I can play better than this!*" he said over and over again, then finally added on the last hole, *"I never have..., but I know that I can!"* Anon.

" I wish I could play my normal game.... just once!" www.com

WHY IS IT "GOLF"?

"However, if we are to consider the appeal of the game it must encompass: the variety and grandeur of the natural setting in which golf is played; man's communion with nature; the healthy benefits he derives from walking down lush green fairways and breathing unpolluted air; the exhilaration he feels from the sharp response of clubhead meeting the ball; the excitement of a golf ball sailing straight at the flag; and the satisfying feeling when an opponent extends his hand in congratulations at a worthy victory." Author unknown.

It is difficult to challenge the theory that at least the best of golf was God's gift to humanity. If in that case, it must then be concluded that the worst of golf, the hazards, traps, out-of-bounds, undulating greens, and the rule of not being able to tamp down spike marks, must have been the Devil's contribution.

WHO STARTED THE MADNESS ANYWAY?

The true origins of golf have not been established with certainty and probably never will be. Arguments on just when and where golf started has raged for many generations and perhaps the whole truth will never be known. Among the many theories offered is one that it was derived from the word *Paganica*, a game played by the Romans that involved striking a feather-stuffed leather ball around open fields. Yet another early stick and ball game which closely resembled golf was *Pall Mall* or *Jeude Mail*, which was originally played in Italy and later adopted by the French and the English.[2] Going back even further, claims have been made that golf was played in China in about 200 BC.

Steven J. H. van Hengal, the late Dutch historian of golf, from research conducted for his book, *Early Golf,* unearthed documents that trace the playing of a game called *colf* on Boxing Day, December 26, in the year 1297. Along with the written reference to the game of colf , van Hengel also found a map of North Holland depicting the "course" with its four "holes" measuring some 4,500 meters!

As a rule, and quite curiously so, each of the various games that are awarded some credit as being among the first versions of golf did *not* involve striking a ball toward a target hole in the ground. While not fully substantiated, credit for this addition to the game has been given to the Scots, with the best estimations of this alternation occurring in the mid 1400s.[2]

A more likely explanation is that golf originated from a game called KET KOVEN played on ice in the European Low Countries (Belgium and Holland) some 500 years ago. The implement used by the players to hit the ball was known as a KOLF a word that simply means CLUB.[3]

The Dutch appear to have the closest ties with golf. As early as the 13th century their literature contained references to "golf-like" games with medieval names such as *Spel Mitten Colve* (play with clubs), *Den bal matta calven te slaen* (to hit the ball with the club) or KOLVEN (club) for short.[4]

However, the Scots contend that the ball used by the people of the Low Countries was about the size of a tennis ball and that since it was hit toward small markers hammered into the ice, the game could not possibly have been what they call GOLF. The common element of the two is that a ball was struck by a STICK.

If one compares the written rather than artistic record, he'd see the first written word of golf in Scotland was James I's edict of 1457 declaring golf illegal. In Holland there was an earlier written record dated 1297. It describes a cross country version of a game with four players to a side, playing four holes with the object being to strike the doors of selected buildings along the way with the ball, the equivalent of "holing out." A barrel of beer went to victors, indicating that celebrating at what is now called "The 19th hole" is a long-standing tradition.[3]

Because there were strong trading ties between the Scots and the people of the Low Countries, there is also a strong argument in favor of the reverse situation – that is to say, the latter took it over and adapted the Scottish game for the ice. As early as the 12th Century, coal mined by Scottish monks was exported to the Low Countries from the harbor of Cockenzie, a small fishing village situated midway along the Firth of Forth. Along this estuary existed what must have been one of the finest strips of golfing constructed in sand dune country. It was here that Scottish golf was born. The area between the sea and the mainland was sandy, common ground – a LINK between the two – which was used by the players and so gave rise to the term GOLF LINKS. Although often used for any golf course, the term should more strictly be applied to those constructed in sand dune country.

The derivation of the word GOLF from its Celtic, and Middle English roots is obscure. The word could have come from the German word KOLBE or the Dutch word KOLF, which both mean club. Some other possibilities are: GLIFF (an incurable madness); GYLF (a notorious liar); GOWFF (a fool or simpleton); GULLF (to beat a shrub with a short stick); GELLVO (horribly; terrible; hopeless; awful); GALFA (my God!; Oh No!); GOULFYL (to cry; to weep); and GAELF (I quit!).

By the 15th Century, golf had been entered into the annals of history, for in 1457 the Scottish Parliament recorded a ban on the games because it was seriously interfering with archery practice. To this day, a regiment of archers march onto the links at Musselburgh and hold an archery tournament. Musselbrugh, the oldest remaining golf course in the world, is just a few miles from Edinburgh and, incidentally, claims to have been the first club to have had a competition for women.

In Edinburgh itself, the historical Leith Links have long since given way to docks and industry. But Leith, too, played an important part in golfing history. Historians claim that it was at Leith that *caddies* got their name – from the young French naval cadets who, in order to earn extra money while their ships were loading, carried the golfer's clubs around the course for the players.

One distinctive British characteristic was the formation of private Golf Clubs. In 1744 the Honorable Company of Edinburgh Golfers had its first meeting and within 100 years there were 30 other clubs in Scotland alone. The "Royal and Ancient Golf Club" was formed in 1754 as the St Andrews Club. In 1897 the same club agreed to become the governing body on the rules of golf, which it still is today. Other countries affiliated themselves to its rules committee, but in 1894 across the Atlantic the United States Golf Association (USGA) had been formed and became the governing authority there.

Like all rules and regulations, those of golf evolved over a long period of time; at one time each golf club has its own. As far as the British were concerned, this situation was resolved when they became the governing body. However, because traditions, conditions and attitudes were somewhat different in the United States, the USGA rules were also different.

To avoid complications and arguments, a joint committee of the British R & A, the American's USGA, and several Commonwealth representatives met in 1951 and produced a unified code, which took effect in 1952. The British and American bodies continue to have joint committee meetings, where changes to the rules are proposed.[3]

Seen on a sign at a Chicago area golf course between an extremely difficult green and the next tee box; *"Remember, this game was invented by the same people who think good music comes from bagpipes."*[4]

THE BIRTH OF THE PGA

In 1879, a well-known Musselburgh caddie, Bob Ferguson, borrowed a few clubs and used them to win his first professional tournament. He was then given a set of eight clubs by a patron and with these he won three British Opens in succession.

It was about this time that a good deal of Britain's most famous courses were being laid out, many of which were designed by the top professionals of the day, who became the resident pro at those clubs. By making clubs, repairing others, giving lessons, selling whatever equipment was available and then playing in challenge matches and competitions, they were establishing an accepted way of life.

The Professional Golfer's Association (PGA) was formed in 1901 when a group met to discuss their dissatisfaction at the way they were being

treated by their clubs. The first PGA tournament was played in October
of that same year at the Tooting Bee Club in South London with the prize
money of 15 English Pounds Sterling.

"RULES OF GOLF" WHO NEEDS EM?

Understanding the Rules of Golf vastly enhances the enjoyment of
playing the game. Golfers must rid the notion that the Rules of Golf must
remain one of life's insoluble mysteries. Knowledge of the Rules makes the
game easier to play and precise, and the correct application often saves a
stroke or two.

The USGA and the R & A of St Andrews established and printed
the Book of Rules of Golf which was then supplemented by formal
interpretations called *"Decisions On The Rules Of Golf"*. These decisions
are responses to questions which defy resolution in the Rules proper. All
of these decisions deal with actual situations from both amateur and
professionals.

Other rules also supplement the Book of Rules of Golf, for instance,
local course rules carry more weight and winter rules are in effect when
deemed necessary by the players or tournament officials. Generally when
playing golf there are three basic principles to follow:

1.   Play the ball as it lies.
2.   Play the course as you fine it.
3.   When it's not possible to do either, do what's fair.

Of course, the question of what is fair leads to some lively debates. The
Rules of Golf are not perfect. On the contrary, every golfer who thinks
about them at all has at least one pet peeve. At the same time, all thinking
golfers must agree that it is a better game if we all use the <u>same</u> rules.

GOLF RULE #1 "ETIQUETTE"

*"Golf etiquette is kind of like the second verse of the national anthem—
good stuff but read by practically nobody."* Herb Graffis[4]

Webster defines ETIQUETTE as "prescribed forms of conduct in a
polite society." Golf a polite society??
The rules of etiquette are simple:

Courtesy on the course – Covers consideration for other players and behavior during play. For example; play without undue delay, let faster players play through when appropriate, get off the green when finished holing out, no one should move, talk, stand to close to, or directly behind another player, and respect honors.

Priority on the course – Two ball matches should be allowed to pass three ball matches, which in turn should be allowed to pass four ball matches. Single players should give way to any match.

Care of the course – Rake bunkers, repair divots, repair ball marks and damage to the green caused by the ball, your clubs or shoes. Golfers should take care not to damage greens by any means, local rules concerning golf carts should be strictly observed and any damage made from practice swings should be repaired, either in the fairway, rough or tee box.

THE UNWRITTEN RULES OF ETIQUETTE[4]

There is more to golf manners than keeping your feet off another player's line of putt. There's a transcendent code golfers acquire only through time and the diligent observation of their more experienced colleagues. This code is violated by mindless, annoying actions, which jar the sensibilities and disrupts the flow of the day's play. Everyone who plays golf and enjoys the game should read the code, learn it and live by it.

Rule 1 On the putting green, mark your ball if it is in another player's field of view. If you lag a putt close, DO SOMETHING WITH IT! Finish by holing out which is your choice or mark it – don't let it just sit there.

Rule 2 Don't ask for putts to be conceded. Always allow your opponent to decide what putts he wants to concede. The next time an opponent of yours asks you, "is this good?" You should reply, "It ain't bad."

Rule 3 Watch every shot from start to finish for every player.

Rule 4 If you're going to complain about your opponent's handicap, wait until after the round to do it.

Rule 5 It's okay to ask your partner for advice but never ask your opponent.

Rule 6 Don't re-stroke a missed putt until everyone else has holed out and rules allow it.

Rule 7 Retrieve your ball from the hole immediately after putting out, and use your hand only. Don't scoop the ball out of the hole with your putter head. You can damage the hole and worse, it looks juvenile.

Rule 8 Never say "Nice Shot!" until the ball has stopped rolling.

Rule 9 If you're keeping score for the group, keep your mind on the game.

Rule 10 Don't offer unsolicited swing instruction.

HERE ARE A FEW PET PEEVES[5]

Player walking off the green while an opponent is putting.

Asking, "Did you really make a 9?" During the 1959 Crosby at Pebble Beach, ABC Announcer Jim McKay was reported to say: *"Now here's Jack Lemmon, about to play the all-important eighth shot."*[1]

Anyone with a cellular phone and using it for any reason other than calling 911, especially when trying to do business while playing with friends or other business associates.

An opponent hits a 3-iron to four feet from the hole then complains he hit it "Thin"

A player refusing a "press" from an opponent on #18 hole.

Hitting a ball "out-of-bounds" from the tee box and immediately teeing another ball up without waiting for the rest of the group to hit first.

Raving and ranting over a missed putt while the other players wait to play their next shot.

Golfers, in anger or for any reason throwing golf clubs.

Any player refusing to rake bunkers after they leave them.

A Golfer counting strokes one at a time while standing on the green.

Someone in the crowd yelling: "You Da Man!"

Golfers who do not repairing their divots or ball marks.

Golfers trying to play, while drunk.

Players driving golf carts while drunk.

Golf carts being driven too close to the green.

And: Players who get mad, at a missed short putt, and attempts to drive the ball off the green with the putter, and takes a four inch divot next to the hole.

EXCEPTIONS TO THE RULES OF GOLF

There is a book written by Henry Beard called "The official EXCEPTIONS to the rules of golf, finally, a rule book that lets you play golf: *Your* way."[6] This is a must read. It covers such items as:

Revisional Ball (Mulligan)
Preferential Ball (Choosies)

Frivolous Ball (Gilligan)
Ball Hit Perfectly Straight (Corrigan)
Ball Teed Up Ahead of the Markers (Moochies)
Ball Swung At and Missed (Practice Swing)
Ball Not Put Fully in Play (Topped Ball)
Audible Interference with Swing (Spookies)
Expendable Ball (Going for it on Doglegs)
Deniable Ball (Nixon)
Nonconforming Shot (Foul Ball)
Causal Air (Windies)
Providential Ball (Found Ball)
Ball Missing in Fairway but Obviously Not Lost (Golf Ball of the Gods)
Wrongful Lie (Unreplaced Divot)
Ground in Flight Outdistancing Ball in Play (Fat Shot)
Ball Hit Under Pressure (Clutch Shot)
Inadvertent Ball (Whoopsies)
Unsolicited Advice as to Choice of Club or Method of Play (Buttinskies)
Unnecessary Rough (Free Kick)
Unreasonable Searches (Boonies)
Ball Hit Slightly Out-of-Bounds (Just a Little Over the Line) and much, much more.

The world's shortest love story about the game of golf:
I hate golf.
I hate golf.
I hate golf.
"Nice Shot."
I love golf.[7]

The Original Rules of Golf
1745
Articles & Laws in Playing at Golf

1. You must Tee your Ball within a Clubs length of the Hole.
2. Your Tee must be upon the Ground.
3. You are not to change the Ball which you Stroke off the Tee.
4. You are not to remove Stones, Bones or any Break Clubs, for the sake of playing your Ball, Except upon the fair Green& that only within a Club's length of your Ball.
5. If your Ball come among watter or any watery firth, you are at liberty to take out your Ball And bringing it behind the hazard and Teeing it, you may play it with any Club and allow Your Adversary a Stroke, for so getting out your Ball.
6. If your Balls be found any where touching one another, You are to lift the first Ball till you Play the last.
7. At Holling, you are to play your Ball honestly for the Hole , and, not to play upon your Adversary's Ball , not lying in your way to the Hole.
8. If you shoud lose your Ball, by it's being taken up, or any other way, you are to go back to the Spot, where you struck last, & drop another Ball, allow your Adversary a Stroke for the misfortune.
9. No man at Holling his Ball, is to be allowed, to mark his way to the Hole with his club or anything else.
10. If a Ball be stopp'd by any person, Horse, Dog, or anything else, The Ball so stopp'd must be played where it lies.
11. If you draw your Club, in order to Stroke & proceed so far in the Stroke, as to be bringing down your Club; If then, your Club shall break in any way, it is to be accounted a Stroke.
12. He whose Ball lyes farthest from the Hole is obliged to play first.
13. Neither French, Dutch, or Dyke, made for the preservation of the Links, not the Scholar's Holes or the Soldier's Lines, Shall be accounted a Hazard, But the Ball is to be taken out, Teed and played with any Iron Club.

John Rattray Cpt.

Verification; The oldest club with documentary proof of its origin is the Company of Gentlemen Golfers now the Honorable Company of Edinburgh Golfers in Muirfield, Scotland. A Silver Club tournament was held in 1745, and the winner, John Rattray became the first captain of the company. The earliest known rules of golf are the 13 recorded by Rattray in the Company's first Minute Book. ENCYCLOPEDIA BRITANNICA, 15th edition, Macropaedia, Volume 8, page 243.

CHAPTER II

"The Verbiage of Golf"

LET'S TALK SOME GOLF TALK

ACE – A hole-in-one. Hitting a ball into the hole from the tee box. Normally by someone who is playing alone. I personally have experienced that momentous occasion. That's the only time I could not find anyone around, not even a course marshal.

Advice – Any counsel or suggestion which could influence a player in determining his play, the choice of a club or the method of making a stroke[8]. Remember, that there is no such thing as little problems, tiny changes, or small pieces of advice.

Back-Door – The opposite side of the cup or hole from the ball position. Sometimes the ball will curve around and enter from the *back-door*. Of course on most occasions, it will choose to go around and wait on the *back-step*, or sit down on the *back-porch* or even go for a nice long roll in the *back-yard*.

Back Nine – The final 9 holes of an 18 hole golf course. While playing in a golf marathon (100 holes in 12 hours), it was said that the first 10 holes were the warm up, while the score that actually counted was on the *back-ninety*.

Backswing – Moving the clubhead away from the ball to a position (somewhere close to having the shaft of the club parallel to the ground) where the normal golfer begins his attack on the ball.

Bail-out - Redirecting the flight path of the ball away from trouble or hazards and in most cases away from the putting surface.

Ballooning – This is where a ball leaves the clubhead in an almost vertical path with very little forward thrust. It comes down with snow on it and is usually equal to about a 280 yard drive, traveling 120 yards up, 120 yards down and 40 yard out. Mostly seen coming from 60 degree wedges or players teeing the ball to high. Also known as *skying*.

Banana Ball - A golf shot with a wood that turns away from the desired flight path in a big outward looping manner. (see: *Slice or Hook*) Golf balls hit this way are last seen entering deep woods, deep grass, deep water or some other kinds of deep do-do.

Best Ball - A competition with 2 or more players to a side or team where medal play (strokes are all counted) is used. Only the best single score on a hole is counted for the team's "Best Ball" score. Some competitions use 2-Best Ball or even 3-Best Ball scoring.

Blind Hole – A hole whose green or putting surface is not visible from the approach shot position (it may be from the tee box or fairway), thereby requiring a player to rely on other senses rather than on the sense of sight, such as the unmistakable _sound_ of an unseen golfer shouting after being struck by your ball, or the distinct _smell_ of trouble, the metallic _taste_ of fear, and the sudden _touch_ of an unknown virus that dictates an immediate return to the club house by way of deep cover.

Block-Out - When, during the forward swing, the body does not rotate far enough past the ball position at impact causing the flight path of the ball to be outward, thus blocking out any chance of getting the ball toward the desired line of flight or away from trouble.

Body English – The leaning, twisting, or other gyrations that players sometimes make, particularly while putting, to "persuade" the ball to go toward and into the hole. If the ball fails to respond to such actions, those movements are often followed by a series of vulgar gestures and physical expressions of disgust referred to as *Body Spanish, Body French,* or *Body Italian.*

Bump and Run - A type of golf shot that is most commonly used on traditional British-style courses. With a bump and run shot golfers aims well short of the intended target and allows for substantial roll to his shot after its initial landing. The majority of American style courses are designed with "Target" golf shots in mind; ones that allow for higher ball flights and less roll.

Carry – The distance that the ball travels in the air. All golfers should know their own ability as to how far a ball will travel when hit by a specific club. When hitting to a green, when another foursome is on that green, *"Fore!!"* is not an excuse for hitting into them, nor is *"So what!"* an apology, and *"Up-Yours!"* is not a proper explanation.[9]

Choke – Miss an important shot or short putt while under pressure. The odds of hitting a duffed shot increases by the square of the number of people watching: $D = nP^2$ or multiplied by the amount of money that can be lost.

Draw - A controlled golf shot that causes the ball to start off line outward (right-to-left for right handed players) but curves back to the line-to-target on purpose,

Drive-for-Show - Long ball hitters that usually do not have a very good short game or are really bad putters or they would win all the tournaments all the time. Exception to this rule may be Tiger Woods. Normally it is the unknown Long-Drive contest winners.

Drop – Normally performed when a legal relief is approved by a tournament official or opponent. The ball is lifted and allowed to drop from the hand while the arm is extended shoulder level to a point within the approved drop area.

Dunch – A low pitch shot.

Fade - A controlled golf shot that causes the ball to start off line inward (left-to-right for right handed players) but curves back to the line-to-target on purpose. Also known as a "cut" or "cut shot."

"You can put "draw" on the ball, you can put a "fade" on a ball, but no golfer can put a "straight" on the ball." www.com

Finesse Shot – Any nonstandard shot used to get the ball out of an awkward or nearly impossible lie by bending, twisting, or stretching the rules or by hitting it directly through a loophole.

Fat-Shot – Also called *Fluffing*. Any stroke made where the clubhead hits the ground before it makes contact with the ball. Usually results in the ball being on line with the hole but very short of the green with the divot lying between the ball and the green.

Flip – A soft, high chip shot.

Flyer (Flier) - A shot that flies substantially longer than desired. Usually as a result of too much grass between the club face and ball when struck from the rough.

Follow-Through - Moving the club head through the ball position and around your body until you're belly button is facing the target. That part of the golf swing that takes place after the ball has been hit but before the club has been thrown.

Tommy Bolt, about the tempers of modern players: *"They throw their clubs backwards and sideways, and that's wrong. You should always throw a club ahead of you so that you don't have to walk any extra distance to get it."*

Foozie (Flub, Muff) - Mishit shots. Since bad shots come in groups of three, a fourth *Foozie* is actually the beginning of the next three *Flubs* to be followed by any number of *Muffs*.

Forward-Swing - Moving the clubhead from the top of the backswing through the ball position toward the target line and onto the *Follow-Through*.

Gimme – A conceded putt usually "*in-the-leather*" (see definition below). *"A gimme can best be defined as an agreement between two golfers...neither of whom can putt very well."* Jim Bishop [9] and *"Remember that it's not a gimme if you are still away." www.com*

Hook – A shot that causes the ball to start on-line to the intended target but then turns away from the intended line in an inward (right-to-left) direction. *Duck Hook*: A shot that starts straight at the target and curves dramatically to the left of the target. *Snap Hook:* A shot that starts out quickly to the left and angles sharply downwards and further to the left. Also been called a "*snipe hook.*" (Term defined for right hand golfers) Pros hit draws, amateurs hit hooks.

Honor – The player who is to play first from the teeing ground[8]. The lowest score on the previous hole has the honor of teeing off first on the next hole. Honor other than on the tee box, is determined by the distance to the pin, the farthest from the hole always has "honors" to hit first, for he is deemed *away.* If after the stroke is taken and the player is still *away,* he still has "honors" providing the option to kick his bag and/or throw the first club.

Inside-Out Swing - When the clubhead crosses the ball position from inside the target line and finishes outside the target line (directional swing plane away from the target).

In-the-Leather - It is the distance from the grip of a standard putter to the edge of the hole when the putter is laid on the ground with the putter head in the hole. In some competitions this is a measurement made to a player's ball to determine if the putt is a *Gimme..*

In-the-Pocket - A player is either holed out or is deemed to be "*out-of-the-hole*" (see below). In either case, his golf ball is in his pocket and not used again until the next hole.

Lag - Getting the ball to a position close to the hole that may be short, left or right on the first putt. Usually the objective of a very long putt or off the green chip shot. The object is to insure that the next putt is easy enough to insure a one putt to hole-out.

Lift – To pick up the ball when a drop is allowed or when special conditions such as wet or soggy weather warrants a player to pick up his ball, clean and place it.

Lob Shot - A high, soft golf shot, generally played near the green with a high-lofted wedge of some type.

Loop or Round - 18 Holes of golf.

Outside-In-Swing - When the clubhead crosses the ball position from outside the target line and finishes inside the target line (directional swing plane away from the target).

Out-of-Bounds – This is bad... It is ground on which play is prohibited and is beyond the boundaries of the course. When the "out-of-bounds" is determined by stakes, posts, fence or a chalk line, the out-of-bound's line is determined to be the nearest inside points of the stakes, posts, fence or chalk line or any other marking device. The line is deemed to extend vertically upwards. A ball is out-of-bounds when all of it lies outside the boundary line.[8] Out-of-bounds is normally the area off the golf course where your ball is considered "lost" which forces you to re-hit the stroke from the original spot of the first shot and take a one stroke penalty, which can be deducted later if your handicap is high enough.

Out-of-the-Hole - When playing match play (strokes are only used to determine who wins each hole in succession not total score) one competitor has either lost the hole or concedes the hole lost to his opponent.

On-the-Tee – A player who is next to tee off.

Past-the-Pin – Any playing area that is behind an imaginary line drawn through the hole, pin, or flag stick extending both left and right.

Penalty Stroke – Any amount of strokes added to the score of a player or side under certain rules[8], such as; out-of-bounds, balls in a hazard, lost balls, or a ball determined to have moved.

Pull – A shot that causes the ball to go on a straight line to an inward direction (left to a right-handed player) away from the target line.

Punch-Out - Low shot played from trees designed to get the ball back into play.

Push – A shot that causes the ball to go on a straight line to an outward direction (left to a left-handed player) away from the target line.

Putt-for-Dough – Good putters, usually the leading money winners.

Quail High - A low shot, either hit accidentally or perhaps on purpose to bore into the wind or beneath limbs of a tree.

Relief – Is spelled *F-r-e-e-D-r-o-p* or moving a ball, without penalty, away from an obstacle, hazard, casual water, or live and deadly animals.

Rub-of-the-Green – It occurs when a ball, in motion, is accidentally stopped or deflected by any outside agency that results in the ball being further from the hole than would normally be expected. It is usually a bad result of a good shot and a bad bounce. *"There are two kinds of bounces: unfair bounces, and bounces just the way you meant to play it." www.com* Sometimes there is a good result from a bad shot, but this is rare indeed. It is also a phrase used in the rules of golf to describe a situation in which the flight of a ball is interrupted by anything other than another player in the match or his or her caddie or equipment. In such incidents the match is continued and the ball is played from wherever it lands unless, whatever accidentally stopped or deflected it: rattles, hisses, spits, growls, snarls, stings, bites, drools; or makes menacing gestures or motions, or circles or makes ready to pounce; or has claws, fangs, a gun, a badge, or a better lawyer than yours.

Sclaff – Onomatopoeic Scottish word for a flubbed shot in which the ground is contacted before the ball is hit. The game's Celtic ventors had plenty of time to develop a rich vocabulary for golfing mishaps, such as a ball topped lightly into the water is called a *FIRKLE*, a ball hit a short distance through dense grass is a *GLEFF*, one that goes straight into the air is a *POOTH*, one hit into the woods is a *LOFONOCK* and one that is hit into other players is a *YEBASTARD*.[10]

Scaffing – Originated in Great Britain, means hitting too far behind the ball—although not in the same manner as a fat shot. A *Sclaff* is almost a good shot but the clubhead does contact the ground before it does the ball.[10]

Scotch Foursome or Twosome - A play where the players will alternate shots. Some competitions alternate after the tee shot others alternate every shot from start to finish.

Scramble – Getting out of trouble and scoring good. It is also the name of specific type of team competition that can have 2 to 6 player to a team. Each member of the team hits a tee shot, then the team decides the better shot. The team then moves all the balls to that spot and hit again. This continues until a ball is holed out. The scoring is a single score for the whole team.

Scruff – To graze the turf with the clubhead, often times resulting is a *Scull* (see below). When you look up to see the results, of this awful shot, you will always look down again at the exact moment when you ought to start watching your ball if you ever want to see it again.

Scull - Hitting the middle of the ball with the bottom edge of the clubhead. Also known as a *bladed shot* resulting in a low trajectory that carries the ball well over the green and into a bunker, lake, or just past the out-of-bounds stakes. When hit from the tee box, it is often referred to as a *Worm Burner*.

Shank - Either hitting the ball on the club head's toe or on the inside of the hosel or neck of the club, causing the ball to go about 90 degrees outward. *Pitch Out or Hoseled Shot* - Slang terms for a *"shanked"* shot.

Slice – A shot that causes a ball to start on line to the target line but then turns sharply away from the target line in an outward direction.

Slog - Definition: *Hit violently with little art.* This we do not want. We learn to swing a club, incorporating a ball strike within that swing.

Smother - Closing the club face at address or hitting down on the ball with an iron with insufficient loft to get the ball into the air.

Square - Clubface, at address, is perpendicular to the target line.

Stance - Taking a stance consist of a player placing his feet in a position for and preparatory to, making a stroke[8]. Also called; addressing the ball.

Stipulated Round - This consists of playing the holes of the course in their correct sequence unless otherwise authorized by the rules committee. The number of holes in a stipulated round is 18 unless a small number is authorized to settle ties or combat the weather. In match play only, the committee may, for the purpose of settling a tie, extend the stipulated round to as many holes as are required for a match to be won.[8]

Stoney It or Stake It - Slang term used to indicate a player hitting the ball close to the hole.

Swing plane – The position of the clubhead and shaft throughout the entire swing. Normally the swing plane has three dimensions. (See a Professional Teaching Pro for any further explanations)

Stymie - A situation, commonly on a putting green, in which one player's ball is directly in the line to the hole of another's. The present Rules allow for the ball in the line to be marked and moved, allowing the player farther from the hole to play without obstruction. Stymie is also the generic term given to a situation when any object is between the player's ball and the hole, blocking the normal play toward the hole. In olden days, the ball in the line of another did not have to be marked and moved, but stayed where it was. It was deemed "the rub of the green" or tough luck for the player who was the farthest from the hole.

Tee Time - It is that time of day when a golfer or a group of golfers are to be on the teeing ground preparing to make the first stroke. It is **NOT** the time to begin discussions or arguments concerning:

1. Bets and their amounts
2. Teams and partners
3. Strokes given or taken
4. Handicaps
5. Old acquaintances or new ones
6. Each stroke of yesterdays round

Through-the-Green - The area of the course except the teeing ground to the back of the putting green on the hole being played and including all the hazards on the course between the tee box and back side of the green.[8]

Tips – The teeing area that is the farthest from the green. The color of the "*Tips*" tee markers are determined by the course but could be black, gold or blue.

Up-and-Down – Holing the ball out from off the green in two strokes: an approach shot and one putt. It is more common for players to go *Up-and-Across, Up-and Beyond, Up-and close, Up-and-around-and-down, Up-and-way-over, Up-and-under, into, though, along, onto, or beside.*

Waggle – Moving your body slightly as address, just prior to the takeaway and backswing.

Whiff or *Fan* - Swinging and missing the ball. (See practice swing)

Wrist-Cocking - During the back swing the wrists should bend normally until at the top. The wrists will have positioned the club shaft parallel to the ground or thereabouts, unless you are John Daly then your club is now vertical to the ground.

Yip or *Yips* – A short stroke or putt that is missed consistently, normally brought on by too much pressure. (See Choke Pg 16)

ITS A WAR ZONE OUT THERE!!

This is what Bob Toski has said about golf, "*non-violent game played violently from within.*" It is amazing how seriously some people take the game, and in the process, they make themselves and others miserable on the course. They get frustrated and angry with themselves and sometimes even end up throwing clubs, ranting and raving, and generally ruining everyone's time. They create violence within.[11]

Why, is a very poor round of golf sometimes referred to as "military golf?" Because a hacker having an extremely wild day off the tee calls to mind a drill sergeant's cadence: "Left-Right-Left-Right!"[11]

Speaking of military golf, why do players yell "fore" to warn of an approaching errant shot? Most experts think the term derives from a warning used by the British Army in battle, formed ranks of infantry at the front with artillery located behind them. Before firing a volley, the artillery yelled "beware before!" to the infantry, who then would lie down to let the cannonballs fly overhead. Shortened to "fore" the term eventually came to be used by golfers to warn other players of errant shots headed their way.[12]

Other terms that may have come from military backgrounds:

Attacking-the-Ball – When a player hits harder at the ball than his normal swing dictates.

Big-Gun – Deep faced driver or favorite driver.

Blast-Out – Hits a shot from a green side bunker (sand trap). The shot is made by hitting the sand about 3 inches in back of the ball which give the appearance of setting TNT and blasting the ball out. It is also referred to as an explosion shot. If the shot is poorly executed, and sufficient amount of sand is not contacted, then the ball flies off the face of the club and the player flies off the handle.

Bombed – A golfer that has been to the nineteenth hole too often.

Break (borrow) – The bend that a ball will take on the green when putted. The shattering of the golf club's shaft by a player, while he is in a fit of rage.

Bunker – Comes from the Scottish word *bonker* meaning a chest or box where coal is kept, usually dug into the side of a hill.[12] A *Bunker* is a hazard consisting of a prepared area of ground that varies in depths and sizes filled with sand or the like. Also call the *Sand Trap* or the *Cat Box*. The margin of the bunker extends downward but not upward. A ball must be touching part of the bunker to be in it.[8] *Pot Bunker* - A small, but very deep bunker, usually filled with sand.

Choking – When a player plays badly due to pressure.

Crunch-a-Drive - Hit a ball a long way off the tee box. Also known as to "*Kill-a-Drive*"

Cut-Shot – A shot where the ball trajectory is higher than normal for a specific club and fades or slices or otherwise moves outward on purpose.

Drop-Area – An area next to a hazard or any designated area allowed for a ball to be dropped after a penalty shot is added or when getting relief from an obstruction.

Explosion – Type of shot played to extricate a ball from a sand bunker. Also called a *blast shot.*

Fire-at-the-Pin – Hitting an approach shot at the pin or flag stick.

Flag-Stick – A long pole with a flag at the top used to mark the position of the hole on the putting surface.

Hit-the-Green - Land your ball on the putting surface with an approach shot.

In Jail - Term used when faced with a difficult shot with little option for hitting towards the green.

Impact-Area – The position on the green or in a fairway where you would like your ball to land. It is also that area on the face of your clubhead that is supposed to come in contact with the ball, known as the *Sweet Spot* (See *Sweet Spot Pg 53 under definition of FACE*).

Killer-Instinct – The ability to beat someone badly without feeling sorry.

Launch angle - The vertical angle of the ball's flight immediately after it leaves the club face.

Marshall - An employee of the golf course, who's job is to keep the rate of play within reasonable limits by being generally unreasonable. Aka: *Ranger* or *Player Assistance.*

Punch-Shot – A low short shot hit with a less lofted club.

Rough – Any grass that is taller than the fairway and first cut off the fairway.

Shot-Gun – A means of starting competition. The tournament players all start playing at the same time on different holes. The start of the tournament is signaled with a shogun blast.

Shot-Pattern – The ball trajectory and landing pattern of a specific club. Could also be called the *Landing Pattern*

Sudden Death - A type of playoff among tied individuals or teams at the completion of a competition. As soon as a team or individual makes the highest score on a hole, they are eliminated from play.

Target Golf - A style of golf played on the preponderance of American tournament courses where a golfer is required to hit a high, lofted approach shot that allows for very little roll to the ball after it lands. This is in contradiction to "Bump and Run" style golf found commonly on British-style, traditional courses. A type of golf competition played at practice ranges wherein golfers compete while shooting to specific targets.

Warbird™ *Sole* - Bi-concave sole design patented by Callaway™ Golf for use on their Big Bertha™ line of woods.

THE GOLFER, HIS EQUIPMENT, AND ASSOCIATES

Equipment – Anything used, worn, or carried by or for the player except his ball in play. Also includes; small objects such as a coin or a tee. A golf cart is equipment of the player whose ball is in involved unless the cart is being moved by another player.[8] Drinking cups and beer cans in a cart can also be deemed as equipment (unless they are empty then see the rules for Loose Impediments).

Hacker (Duffer) - A novice player or beginner. A player with a very high handicap that takes *divots* the size of a *"Snatch of Haugh"* (see divots below) hence is seen as hacking his way around the course.[12]

Caddie – A person who carries or handles a player's equipment during play and otherwise assists him in accordance with the rules.

Forecaddie – A person employed by the rules committee to indicate to players the position of the balls on the course and is considered an *outside agency*.[8]

Partner – He is a player associated with another player on the same side or team[8]. In a threesome, foursome or a four-ball where the context so admits, the player shall be held to include his partner.

He's the match play team member who holes out from a bunker to score a birdie on a hole that you are about to win with a tap-in par, then 4 putts from 12 feet for a triple bogey on a hole where you lie six and your ball is still 10 feet from the hole.

Referee – A person who has been appointed by the rules committee to accompany players to decide questions of fact and of golf law. He shall act on any breach of the Rules or Local Rules which he may observe or which may be reported to him by an observer.[8]

Marker – A coin or other round object used to mark the position of the ball on the green. In the USA, only round flat objects may be used for ball markers (this rule has been changed and can include a tee). Any off shaped object such as a room key, putt head, dead leaf, etc. used to mark a ball will result in a one stroke penalty. It is also a *scorer* in medal or stroke play who is appointed by the rules committee to record a competitor's score[8.] He may also be a fellow competitor. He is not a referee. A marker should not lift a ball or mark its position unless authorized to do so by the competitor and, unless he is a fellow competitor, should not attend the flag stick or stand at the hole or mark its position.

Observer – An official appointed by the rules committee to assist a referee to decide questions of fact and to report to him any breach of a Rule or Local Rules. An observer should not attend the flag stick, stand at or mark the position of the hole, or lift the ball or mark its position.[8]

Divot – The colorful Scottish word for a piece of turf scooped up from the ground in front of the ball (or behind the ball, see *hacker*) in the course of hitting a golf shot. In Scotland, depending on its size, a divot is referred to as a; *Wee Tuftie* (2" X 4"), *Peg O' Sward* (4" X 6"), *Snatch of Haugh* (6" X 8"), *Fine Tussock* (8" X 10"), *Glen* (10" X 14"), *Firth* (1.5' X 3'), *Lock* (2' X 4'), and a *Damned English Divot* (anything larger than 8 feet square).[12]

Rain-Suit – Water proof coat and pants set worn during wet, damp or cold weather, without a tie.

Side and Matches –

1. *Side*: A player, or two or more players who are partners.
2. *Single*: A match in which one plays against another.
3. *Threesome*: A match in which one plays against two and each side plays one ball.
4. *Foursome*: A match in which four players play against one another, each playing his own ball.
5. *Best-Ball*: A match in which one plays against the better ball of two others or the better ball of three. A better combined score of a team against a better combined score of another.
6. *Four-Ball*: A match in which two play their better ball against the better ball of two other players.

Foursome – Four players playing a round together, each against the others[8.] Three are a *Threesome* and two are a *Twosome*. Four golfers playing slowly are a *Gruesome*. Four men playing after a liquid lunch at the 19th hole are a *Fearsome*. A single attractive lady playing alone is a *Toothsome* also could be known as a *Troublesome*. A husband and wife is a *Quarrelsome*. A group of golfers giving advice to others are a *Meddlesome*. A player with a lot of old jokes is a *Tiresome*. Two younger players playing a fast, sub-par round are a *Loathsome*. Statement of fact: Whenever you play in a mixed foursome, there will always be at least one hole where you have to hit your second shot before the ladies tee off.

Leader Board – The billboards (some electronic) around the course and clubhouse that depict the current tournament leaders on which your name never appears.

Retriever – An instrument with a telescoping shaft used to retrieve golf balls from a water hazard or backyards of houses lining the fairways containing big dogs.

Stimpmeter – A grooved bar used to measure the speed of the greens. A ball is placed on the bar which is raised until the ball rolls freely. The distance that the ball rolls on the green is measured and the operation repeated several times, with an average being taken.[9]

Golf Bag - The bag containing all the clubs, balls, and other items used by the golfer to play with.

Golf Cart - A device with wheels that provides a means of moving the golf bag around the course without carrying it. It can be motorized or pull type.

Practice Tee – Also known as the *Driving Range*. A place where a player can go to convert his nasty hook into a wicked slice.

Tee - A wooden or plastic peg or any other device used to elevate the ball from the ground while hitting from the tee box. It must not be longer that 4 inches (101.6mm) long and must not be designed or manufactured in such a way that it could indicate the *line of play* or influence the movement of the ball[8]. The term probably comes from the Scottish word *Teay*; a small pile of sand. For many years golfer would make a pile of sand or dirt and place the ball on it for driving. In 1920, Dr. William Lowell, a Boston dentist, invented the wooden tee to prevent his hands from being scratched. [12]

Turn - The halfway point of any 18 hole golf course.

CHAPTER III

"A Little Space and Time"

THE GOLF COURSE

Jimmy Demaret speaking to Robert Trent Jones: *"Trent, I've seen a course you'd really like. You stand on the first tee and take an unplayable lie."*[1]

Golf courses started as LINKS, just as Mother Nature created. As time passed, a few additions were made by players, although really no thought was given to design. In the latter part of the 19th century, improvements were restricted to the construction of formal flat greens and ramparts of bunkers.[3]

Slowly, however, more imagination was used and a breed of golf course architects emerged. At one time the number of holes on a golf course varied, some were 19 while others were 20, and 22 but in 1764 the course at St. Andrews was decreased from 22 to 18 holes and this became the norm.

The way I heard it was that the number 22 was established because there are about 33 ounces of liquid in a Scottish quart (liter) of whisky. Since a jigger or shot of whisky, consumed on each tee box, was about 1.5 ounces, it should take 22 holes of golf to finish the bottle. Of course when the whisky was gone, there was no good reason to continue to play. I imagine that in reality, trial and error, and due to spillage and hearty drinkers, the number of swallows that were actually derived from a fine Scotch liter of Whisky was 18.

Golf Course – The whole area within which play is permitted. It is the duty of the committee to define the boundaries accurately.[8]

> *"The shortest distance between any two points on a golf course is a straight line that passes directly through the center of a very large tree." www.com*

Links – A golf course designed for a seaside terrain. Also a golf course laid out with nine holes leading away from the club house and other nine holes leading back to the club house. Another definition fits all golf courses since all the holes are "Linked" together like a string of wieners.

Loop – A round of golf (18 holes) on a 9 holes-out and 9 hole-in links course.

Teeing Ground – Also called the Tee Box. This is the starting place for all the holes to be played. It is defined as a rectangular area with the depths of a side equals two golf clubs in length. The front edge of the tee box is defined by a line drawn from the front of the tee markers. A ball is outside the teeing ground when all of it lies outside the stipulated area[8]. When playing the first stroke with any ball from the teeing ground, the tee markers are immovable obstructions. This area is considered by Colorado and probably many other states to be a safe area where a golfer can be reasonably assured of not being hit by an errant shot. If he is hit while on the tee box, the golfer whose ball hit him could be found negligent and liable.

Teeing – In teeing, a ball may be placed on the ground, on an irregularity of surface created by the player with sand or other substances in order to raise it off the ground.

First Tee – See the definitions under: CHOKE; FLUFF, HOOK, SCAFF, SHANK, SLICE, WHIFF, BALLOONING, or MULLIGAN.

Fairway - The short grasses area between the tee box and the putting surface (green) that all golfers have seen but few actually use.

> *"You can hit a 2-acre fairway 10% of the time, and a 2-inch rough 90% of the time." www.com*

Green – The extra short grassed area called the *Putting Surface or Putting Green*[8]. This is where the hole is and its color matches the color of money, of which this is where most of it is made or lost. The ball is deemed to be on the *Green* if any part of the ball is touching it.

Carpet – A term used to describe the *Putting Green or* to describe the *Approach* or first cut of grass in front of the *Green*.

Collar – The first cut around the *Green*. Also referred to at times as the *Apron*, *Fringe* or *Frog-Hair*. It is the area of grass that borders a putting green and is typically higher than the grass on the green, but lower than the grass on the fairway. The area from which a tricky, easily flubbed shot is made, sometimes called a *Chupp* or a *Putch* (half chip, half pitch shot) or simply a *Chitt* shot.

Cup – A plastic cylinder fitted into a hole in the *Green*. Strictly speaking, it is only the liner of the hole. Regular golf usage player will often say *Cup* when they mean *Hole* just as they frequently will say *just in bounds* when they mean *out-of-bounds, Oh here it is* when they mean *I can't find it* and *five* when they mean *seven*.

Hole – The "*Hole*" is 4 and ¼ inches (108 mm) in diameter and at least 4 inches (101.6mm) deep, containing a plastic liner called the *Cup*. The cup is sunk at least 1 inch below the putting surface unless the nature of the soil around it makes it impractical to do so[8]. It should be noted for those golfers that like to putt to a position 18 inches past the hole, that the speed of the ball approaching the hole will effectively reduce the size of the hole by half or even as much as a three quarters. (See chapter on putting for explanation).

Lip or *Rim* – The perimeter of grass surrounding the hole. *Lip* may also be the remarks made by fellow players when your ball stops on the *Rim* or hits the holes and spins out to the left or right, or when the ball hangs on the *Lip* of the hole for 9 seconds before falling in.

Flagstick – A moveable straight pole indicator provided, with or without bunting or other material attached, centered in the *Hole* and *Cup* to show the hole's position on the *Green*. It is to be round and never square.[8]

Clubhouse – The place where the local rules are posted.

Committee – Those in charge of the competition or, if the matter does not arise in a competition, they are in charge of the course.[8] The authorized drafters of the local rules and who are in charge of the course of play.

Competition – The form of play established by the local rules.

Course – The area of play where the local rules are in effect.

Courtesy – The type of conduct specifically mandated by the local rules.

Crapola – Local Rules.

Cop – A knoll or bank regarded as a hazard or obstacle.

Dimples – Mounds in the fairway or on the *Green* or on the golf ball.

Hog-Backs – Small mounds or hills in the fairway or on the *Green*.

Dog-Leg – A hole with a turning fairway between the tee and the *Green*. A hole with a pot-marked tea area, unkempt fairways, and a patchy *Green* is said to be *Dog-Eared*. A hole in which large amounts of casual water accumulates is a *Dog-Paddle*. A hole with an elevated tee box and *Green* with a sunken, treacherous approach is a *Dog-Dish*. Any course on which holes like the aforementioned are predominate simply called a *Dog*. Any golf ball that does not respond in an appropriate manner to proper verbal commands like: *Go in*!!, *Bite*!!, or *Stop*!! is also known as a *Dog*. Having a bad day on the course is a *Dog-day-Afternoon*. Finally, having more handicap than your ability dictates especially when it is higher than the sandbagger your playing is having a *Leg Up* on the competition.

Hazards – A bunker, water hazard, or lateral water hazard[8]. Bare patches, scrapes, roads, tracks, or paths are not hazards. *"Hazards attract; fairways repel." www.com*

A *"Bunker"* is an area of bare ground, often a depression which is covered with sand (although there are grass bunkers too). Grass covered areas with the sand bunker are not considered to be part of the bunker. Refer back to the definition of *Sand Trap*.

A *"Water Hazard"* – is any sea, lake, pond, river, ditch, surface drainage ditch, or other open water courses (regardless of whether or not it contains water), and anything of similar nature. All ground or water within the margin of the water hazard, whether or not it be covered with any growing substance is part of the water hazard. The margin of the water hazard is deemed to extend vertically upwards and defined by yellow stakes or lines.

A *"Lateral Water Hazard"* – is a water hazard or that part of a water hazard so situated that it is not possible or is deemed impractical to drop a ball behind the water hazard and keep the spot, at which the ball last crossed the margin of the hazard, between the player and the hole. The lateral water hazard is defined by red stakes or lines and deemed to extend vertically upwards.

Casual Water – It is any temporary accumulation of water which is visible before or after the player takes his stance and is not in a water hazard. Snow and ice are either casual water or loose impediments, at the options of the player.[8] *Tears,* however, no matter how copious, do not constitute casual water.

> *"I've had a good day when I don't fall out of the golf cart!"*
> Buddy Hackett

Ground-Under-Repair – Any portion of the course so marked or so declared. It includes material piled up for removal or a hole made by the greens keeper, even if it is not so marked[8] Stakes and lines defining such areas are deemed in or part of the area. Grass cuttings and other material on the course which have been abandoned and are not intended to be removed are not ground-under-repair unless so marked.

Rough – Everything else on the course not described above. It is the naturally wild areas bordering the fairway and sometimes separates the fairway from the tee box. There are three basic types of rough:

> *Low Rough* – A narrow strip of 1 to 3 inch-high grass where the ball may be easily playable, usually called the *first cut* off the fairway.

Primary Rough or Second Cut – Deep rough past the first cut off the fairway.

Third Cut - A section of rough, generally found on tournament courses that borders the second cut. The third cut is very severe and may not be found on all but the most difficult courses.

Dark Rough – Where the ball may be eaten or kept for use as an object of worship by small primitive people.

Tiger Country – Heavy, deep and *Dark Rough*. Also, the back tees, called the *"tips"* (sometimes the tee markers are colored gold or black) located around 20 to 40 yards behind the normal white or blue tees from which the fairway can be seen through a small narrow tunnel of trees.

Barranca – Rocky gully or water course.

Local Rules – A set of regulations established by a rules committee that are ignored only by players on one specific course rather than by golfers as a whole.

Freak – Contrary to the traditions or rules of golf.

Golf Lawyer - A player that makes pettifogging use of the rules.

Loose Impediments – Are natural objects such as stones, leaves, twigs, branches, and the like, dung, worms, insects, and the casts or heaps made by them, provided they are not fixed or growing, are not solidly embedded and do not adhere to the ball. Sand and loose soil are *loose impediments* on the putting green, but not elsewhere. Snow and natural ice, other than frost are either *causal water* or *loose impediments*, at the option of the player. Dew and frost are not loose impediments.[8] Some objects deemed as loose impediments include: half-eaten pears, apples, bananas, or other fruit skins, ant hills, dead sea crabs, fallen trees that are not attached to the trunk, aeration plugs, clods of dirt, and gravel.

Obstructions – Anything artificial, whether erected, placed, or left on he course, including the artificial surfaces and sides of roads, paths but excluding:

1. Objects defining out-of-bounds, such as walls, fences, stakes, and railings.
2. In water hazards, artificial surfaced banks, or beds, including bridge supports when part of such bank. Bridges and bridge supports which are not part of such a bank are obstructions.
3. Any construction declared to be an integral part of the course.[8]
4. An *obstruction* is a *moveable obstruction* if it may be moved without unreasonable effort, without unduly delaying play or without causing damage and can be replaced in its original position or condition. Otherwise it is an *unmovable obstruction.*

Outside Agency – Any agency not part of the match or, in stroke play, not part of a competitor's side, and includes a referee, a marker, an observer, or a forecaddie. Neither wind nor water is an outside agency.[8]

Summer Rules - Term given to standard USGA Rules' play. Ball must be played as it lies except on putting greens and teeing grounds.

PLAYING TIME

The pace of golf is unique and in obvious contrast to that of most sports. In golf, you have too much time to think which, is the biggest handicap for most players. Between shots a negative train of thoughts can become entrenched and it seems like an endless time to over analyze and become confused, discouraged, and angry.

Do you realize that during a full 18 holes of golf with a score of 90, you only swing a club for about 8 to 12 minutes? That's if you take a lot of practice swings. The rest of the time (about 4 hours) is spent on analyzing, agonizing, making decisions as to distance, club selection, swing or for looking for your ball. The ball, by the way just sits there and the pace of the game demands that the golfer be at an intense peak of concentration during a few seconds of the swing, supremely challenging his ability to keep from being detracted during the long intervals between shots. One should avoid this time to over analyze your play, to berate yourself, to study the scoreboard, to determine the cut, or to entertain any other such thoughts.

You can conclude from this that the walk between shots is one of the most critical parts of the game. It is most often that in the interval between shots is where the inner (success) and the outer (denial) games are won and lost. The winners or good golfers learn to use this time between shots to relax and to prepare mentally for the total concentration he will need during the 4 to 6 seconds of his next swing routine.

TIME AND SPEED OF PLAY

The Rules of Golf provided by the USGA states in rule 6 – 7: "*The player shall play without undue delay. Between completion of a hole and playing from the next teeing ground, the player shall not unduly delay play.*"

Slow play is not very well accepted or tolerated by most golfers, and is becoming a serious problem. With the increase of the number of golfers and the limited number of golf courses and tee times being available, the time it takes to play an 18 hole round of golf has increased. Where it used to take only 3.5 hours for a foursome (riding in carts) to complete a round, it now takes from 4.5 to 5 hours on an average, to complete a round of golf on a public course, depending on how many golfers are allowed on the course due to tee time intervals.

Professionals are penalized for undue delays but in most cases amateur players are not. More and more exclusive clubs and public courses are attempting to keep the speed of play within limits by providing a course marshal (also known as the "*players assistance*") to monitor and observe play, but that is not the solution to the problem of slow play. Two primary reasons for long drawn out rounds: 1) Courses are putting players on the course every 8 minutes while it takes, on an average, 12 to 15 minutes to play a hole on a overcrowded course, and; 2) golf is probably the only sport that there are no rules or prerequisites or consequences to govern play for the slow play of beginner players, high handicap players or just plain slow players.

I believe that all players should have some type of instruction on: how to play the game; course rules; rules of etiquette; rules and regulations governing play according to the PGA; and awareness that their play does affect other players around, in front and primarily behind them.

I am not against new or beginning golfers or high handicappers, but I am against any level of golfer playing without respect for the course or other players. Players that do not care or just simply don't realize how much time they take on a course or how much damage they do to the greens and fairways should not be allowed to play until they have learned the basic fundamentals of the game. As a golf instructor and one time professional, I want to encourage people to become golfers but I want them to realize that golf has responsibilities, it requires respect for other players as well as the course. They should also realize that their attitudes and actions reflect their self discipline and how it affects the play and enjoyment of other players.

As individuals, here are a few things we can do to speed up play:

* Concentrate and plan ahead. Be thinking about your next shot.
* Be prepared to play when it's your turn... select your club in advance, line up your shot or study your line while others are making their shots. <u>When it's your turn, be ready</u>.
* Drive or walk directly toward your ball or on the same line that your ball took.
* Carry a spare ball and take no mulligan. Be ready to play a provisional ball.
* Limit your number of practice swings or take your practice swings while others are making their shots, provided that it does not interfere with their play
* Don't walk beyond your ball for more than a few paces and only to look for yardage markers.
* Watch your ball and the balls hit by the other players until they have come to a complete stop. Mark a line of flight of the ball if ball is out of sight before stopping.
* Be realistic about hitting to a green or off the tee box. Usually the "waiters" can not hit a ball that far even with the help of two other players.
* Learn how far you can hit a ball with specific irons and woods.
* When you are out of a hole or hitting a triple bogie, pick up, if you're not in competition.
* Mark you score card after you walk off the green or while you're on the next tee box.
* Learn the rules and plan to play by them.

Groups can speed up play by:

* Forget honors. The first man ready to hit, do so. First man to hole-out should proceed to the next tee box and tee-off.
* Putt when ready, be ready to putt. If everybody lines up their putts together it saves time.
* Shorter hitters play first from the tee box.

* If there is a hole or space open ahead of you, let the group behind play through, then keep up with them.
* Only one man looks for his ball in the rough and for only 2 - 3 minutes. The others should be getting ready and indeed begin to hit their next shot.
* Wave up the following group on par-3s, particularly if the next tee box is occupied. You can be putting out as they approach the green and it gives the group that is on the next tee, time to hit.

What courses can do:

* Allow carts on all the fairways even if only with the 90 degree rule.
* Ban winter rules during tournaments but allow preferred lies (moving the ball while in the fairway especially from divots or sanded areas with the club head so it can be hit easier).
* Use marshals or "player assistants" to govern speed of play.
* Place pins in on the side of the green closest to where the next tee box is. Especially during weekend play when the course is full.
* Encourage lead groups to ride in motorized carts. They set the time and speed of play.

Remember: The game of golf is immediately behind the group ahead, not immediately ahead the group behind.

CHAPTER IV

"The Real Reason For Playing Golf"

KEEPING SCORE AND WINNING BETS

In all sport games, competition means nothing unless there is a way to see who is doing better. The means used in most sports is assigning value to specific actions and then comparing the totals at the end of the competition. This is how one can tell who won and who didn't.

In golf, each *stroke* (see definition below) is counted as one attempt to strike the ball. Remember the "Short Story About Golf" on page xv? The object is to strike the ball as few times as possible while moving the ball from tee to hole. The least amount of strokes in doing so wins and is the best, while those who lose, as a consolation, got to play more golf and get to see more of the golf course and the surrounding areas.

In the game of golf, scoring is sometimes relative. For example, in football and baseball the team that scores the most points wins. There are no points (handicap) "given" to the weaker or poorer playing team to even up the competition. Whereas in golf, all levels of golfers can play competitive games because of an equalizer called the "Colt 45", I mean the "Handicap" although both of these items can be very deadly at times. *To some golfers, the greatest handicap is the ability to add correctly." www.com*

Now, duffers, pros, ladies, kiddies of all sizes and shapes can play and compete because strokes can be deducted from their score because they are not as good as the scratch golfer (that guy who shoots par all the time). The handicap system is a good idea, if it weren't for people abusing it. But, it's human nature to want to win all the time, even if it means cheating to do it. *"In golf, some people tend to get confused with all the numbers... they shoot a "six" yell "fore" and write "five"." www.com "Golf appeals to the idiot in us and the child. Just how childlike golfers become, is proven by their frequent inability to count past five."* John Updike.

THE HANDICAP[13]

The handicap system was established so that all golfers can compete with each no matter the level of skill of individual golfers. It was established to equalize the scores for amateur tournaments and is based on 80% of the average score posted for the lowest ten scores of the last twenty rounds of 18 holes played.

In 1994, the USGA introduced a simple, straightforward, and easy-to-remember procedure to adjust scores under Equitable Stroke Control (ESC). Under this system is described the way you are required to adjust your score or set a maximum number that a player can post on any hole dependent on the player's current course handicap. This system is designed to keep the handicaps at a more reasonable level for all golfers and to keep players from scoring a high number on a just few holes to "pad" their handicap and take unfair advantage of other players (see Sandbagger).

TERMS USED IN SCORING

Albatross (Double Eagle) - A score of three under par (a 2 on a par 5).

Birdie – One stroke less than or under par. *"Every time a golfer makes a birdie, he must subsequently make two triple bogeys to restore the fundamental equilibrium of the universe." www.com*

Bogey – A score of one stroke more than or over par. This is the number of strokes needed to finish a hole by a golfer of average skill and above-average honesty. According to Stephen Leacock, a Canadian writer of yesteryear, *bogey* is an imaginary player who does each hole of golf in the fewest strokes that a first-class player with ordinary luck ought to need for that hole. Most score cards will have a multitude of bogeys, a few buzzards and even some triple bogeys on one or more holes, especially if the score is kept by other players. The term comes from an imaginary *Colonel Bogey* of the Great Yarmouth Club in England. It is believed that a Major Charles Wellman, while playing against *ground score* (par), referred to failing to get par as *getting caught by the bogey man*, a phrase from a popular eighteenth-century tune. The members of the club began referring to an imaginary new member, *Colonel Bogey*, who would always shoot even par. As the game spread to the United States, *bogey* was narrowed to represent a score of one over par on a hole[11].

Buzzard – A double bogey or a score of two strokes more than or over par.

Eagle – A score of two strokes less than or under par. (1 on a par 3, 2 on a par 4, 3 on a par 5)

Gimme – When a ball is close or around the hole is such proximity that an opponent or other player will concede that the putt can be easily made and "gives" the putt to the player. The ball is deemed to be holed out and can be picked up without making another stroke but still counting one additional stroke on the score.

Gobble – A putt that hit the back edge or rim of the hole, jumps in the air about 6 inches or so and then falls into the hole.

Handicap – It is a scoring system that allows certain golf players to deduct strokes from their scores because they need to win all the tournaments they play in.

Par – Normal or average score for a golf hole. Normally, it is determined by the length or yardage or difficulty of a hole. On the average, plus or minus a few yards, Par 3's are up to about 230 yards long, Par 4's are up to about 480, Par 5's are longer. On rare occasions, there are some par 5's and 6's that reach as far as 650 + yards. I remember one such hole, par 6 listed at 650 yards, located in South Korea that played up hill to an immense blind green.

Putt – A golf stroke on the putting surface after everything else has failed to put the ball in the hole.

Putts – The number of strokes taken on the putting surface.

Putz – The player trying to put the ball in the hole, usually having putts of four or more and still insisting on lining up the next (4th or 5th) putt from both sides of the hole.

Sandbagger – A person whose handicap indicates that he couldn't possible have played as well as he just did to win the tournament.

Stroke – The forward movement of the club made with the intention of fairly striking at and moving the ball.[8]

Tap-in – A putt short enough to miss one handed but not close enough to qualify as a *gimme.*

Terms in Reckoning in a Match - In match play (see definition below), the reckoning of holes is kept by the following terms:

1 – *So many holes up –* Winning by a certain number of holes.
2 – *So many holes down –* Losing by a certain number of holes.
3 – *Out of the hole –* In match play or best ball, a player whose score could not help or win the hole.
4 – *Dormie –* In match play, when a player is losing by the number of holes that are left to play.

Match Play - Hole by Hole competition. Low score on a hole wins the hole. The player winning the most holes wins the match even though he may have a higher total stroke score.

Medal Play – Total stroke scoring. The lowest number or fewest strokes wins.

Mulligan - An extra shot allowed by agreement between players that is not necessarily scored or if scored, the previous shot is not. The term *Mulligan,* at first was thought to mean *maul it again* but it turns out that it actually came from the name of an Anglo-Irish aristocrat and passionate golfer who was born in May 1793 in a modest manor house called Duffnaught Hall. Thomas Mulligan was the man who tamed the first tee (see definition on page 31) and became famous for it. It is not really known if he authored all of the following but no matter, they apply just as the MULLIGAN does.

a. The score the player reports on the first hole should be regarded as his first opening offer.

b. If you really want to get better at golf, go back and take it up at a younger age.

c. There is no such thing as a friendly wager.

d. Never leave your opponent with the sole responsibility for thinking of all the things that might go wrong with his shot.

e. Four days of perfect golf weather begins on Monday.

f. There is no ground that couldn't use a little repair.

g. Don't play with anyone who would question a 7.

h. Strokes always accumulate faster than they can be forgotten.

i. The statute of limitations on forgotten strokes is two holes.

j. It's often necessary to hit a second drive to really appreciate the first one.

k. Nonchalant putts count the same as chalant putts.

l. Good sportsmanship is as essential to the game of golf as good penmanship is to stock car racing.

m. The people on the greens keeping staff always look like they took the job because a golf course is such a good place to dispose of bodies.

"Through the years of experience I have found that air offers less resistance than dirt." Jack Nicklaus[12]

SIDE BETS AND OTHER WAYS TO LOSE MONEY

Lee Trevino: *"You can make a lot of money in this game. Just ask my ex-wives. Both of them are so rich that neither of their husbands work."*

Nassau – A three way bet. Stroke total for the first nine holes, a second nine hole total, and the total for the full eighteen holes. It can be match and/or medal play.

Press – An extra bet initiated during match play when one player become two holes down. The bet is a second bet covering the remaining holes of the nine or the eighteen.

Air-press – A press bet or a double bet made after the ball has been struck and is still in the air.

No-Bogey – Usually within a foursome with handicaps, a bet where any player that can play a complete round without a bogey of any kind wins the pot or a share of it.[14]

Hammer – A doubling of a bet at any time during the play of a hole. You can hammer your opponent as many times as you want or until he knocks your block off.

Rabbit – A game that is similar to the "Skins" game. The rabbit is designated as the first player in a group to beat all the others on a hole. He stays the rabbit, and wins each succeeding hole (not preceding holes which makes it different from the skins game), until one or more of the other members of the group beats him. A new rabbit is designated only when a single players beats the rabbit being chased or beats the group as a whole. If no new rabbit is designated, the remaining holes have no winner.

Greenie – Getting your ball closest to the pin on a par 3 hole. You can also win a *Sandie* (up and down from a sand trap), or a *Barkie* (up and down after hitting a tree). Birdies also qualify in this type of betting. Some more difficult bets to win are the *Sloushie* (getting a par from a water hazard), an *Outtie* (par a hole after hitting a shot out-of-bounds), a *Whiffie* (par a hole after completely missing the ball on the tee box), the *Cabinie* (par a hole after hitting a house that is out-of-bounds and bouncing back into play), and the not so famous but ever so dreaded *Wienie* (par a hole after a short legged dog steals your ball and you are forced to take one penalty shot).

BBB – *(Bingo – Bango – Bongo)* - Also called bingle-bangle-bongle [11] The game is played where three bets can be won on each hole. *Bingo* is "the first on the green from" , *Bango* is the "closest to the pin", and *Bango* (the first in the hole).

Skins – In a *skins* game players compete on each hole to be the lowest score posted for that hole. He is said to have skinned the other players. If any two players tie for the lowest score on a hole, then there is no winner for that hole and the amount of money that hole is worth is carried over and added to the value of the next hole. The carry over continues until one player wind the skin. This is also called *scats* or *syndicates*[5]. The term *skins* goes back to the days when a hunter displayed his success by the number of pelts or *skins* he had upon returning from the hunt.[12]

"Never bet with anyone you meet on the first tee who has a deep suntan, a 1-iron in his bag, and squinty eyes." Davey Marr[16]

Daffinitions

Ballenwaller - A golf ball covered in mud or other brown sticky stuff that cannot be cleaned off but must be played as is, according to the rules. See *crapola* under "Local Rules".

Clubsidy – A bonus (par or birdie) provided by a wrong club selection, swung in an incorrect manner, attributing to an unconventional ball strike, resulting in a ball flight "over hill and dale, through the woods and on to gramma's house" located on the green a foot from the hole.

Fibrillation – Uncontrolled twitching of individual muscular fibers of a golfer hand when posting a known incorrect score for the purpose of raising one's handicap or winning a bet.

Glovely – The use of a golf glove that does not fit properly but provides excellent excuses for a disastrous round of golf.

Goofoffer – A mistake made prior to a golf swing such as a wrong club selection, swing alignment, or a lack of concentration, that generally results in a terrible golf shot. It is a "goof" "offered" as a substitution for a normal or good swing.

Iltamper – A Golfer using a putter to illegally tapping down a *"Spike's Peak"* (See definition below)

Imputtlaxitor – A golfer that is unable to putt with a quality of being unconcerned.

Prolaggard - A notoriously slow player.

Puttlaxing – Putting while showing little of no concern of the outcome or result.

Scafface – A hole-in-one using scaffing. (See page 20)

Spike's Peak – A Colorado Springs term for a very tall spike mark located one inch in front of your ball directly in your putting line that by rule you cannot be an iltamper. (See definition of Iltamper above)

Subteer – A golfer whose golf ball, after several tries, keeps falling off the tee on the first hole.

Taboot – The prohibited act of moving a golf ball with a golf shoe still attached to the golfer so as to improve the lie of the ball.

CHAPTER V

"It's What We Play With"

GOLF CLUBS AND DEFINITIONS

Golf Club or *Stick* – Not really either, but an instrument designed to move the golf ball in a desired direction and a desired flight path. Added definitions include: any instrument wrapped around a immovable object such as a tree is a *smashie*. If it is flung into a water hazard it is a *splashie*. If it is used to pile-drive a tee into the ground after a player couldn't use it to hit a ball with, its a *bashie*. If used to fend off dogs fending off players getting their lost ball from their yard, it is a *Lassie*. A club that was allegedly used to make a Hole-in-One is a *fibstick* and if the same club was a wood rather than an iron it was a *fablespoon*.

Iron – A instrument with thin flat metal bladed head used for hitting the golf ball in a multitude of directions and distances. They come in different sizes and shapes and usually in a set, consisting of several (up to 12 in a set) lofts and head sizes. The lower the number on the iron the lesser loft the hitting area will have, and the longer the shaft from grip to head. There are two distinct types of irons, the *cavity back* and the *blade*. They are both made from a steel compound and are either forged (stamped) or casted (made from a mold). There are some irons made from a brass compound and some from a Beryllium copper alloy but mostly steel.

Muscle Back – Refers to a forged iron, normally a blade type that has bulges or ripples on the back of the club head opposite the hitting area.[12]

Woods – An instrument whose head is made from wood or metal or some other compound and is thick and rounded. They come in different lofts and numbers which designate the use, such as the 1-wood is a driver. The lower the number the less loft of the hitting area. Other definitions of *woods* are:

1. It is a type of golf club used to hit a golf ball a long distance or pile-drive a short tee deep into the tee box.
2. It is the area where the golf ball lands after being hit a long distance just before the tee is pile-driven into the tee box.

"I'm hitting the woods just great, but I'm having a terrible time getting out of them." Harry Toscanno[16]

Fairway Wood – A medium lofted *wood* (see above) used to get a ball out of a good lie in the fairway and into position for a shot to the green from a sand trap, a steep slope, a deep grass bunker, water hazard, or from in back of a tree.

"HAND YOU A WHAT?" SAID THE CADDIE

"The only thing in my bag that works is the bug Spray" Bruce Lansky

Bakspin – Term given to hickory shafted clubs which contain large grooves in their faces.

Baffy – The older name for a 5-wood.

Baffy-Spoon – A more lofted wooden club, like a wedge.

Blaster – A sand wedge. The nickname for a 1-Wood or a Driver.

Brassie – A club (normally a 2-wood) that got its name from a Brass plated sole on bottom of club head..

Bulger – A driver or 1-wood with a slightly more convex in the face than normal.

Carruthers – Designer of the first club with the bore-through hosel design; specifically related to older hickory shafted clubs.

Chipper – An iron like a wedge, used to hit the ball to the green from short distances. It can cause a golfer to babble (one of the dictionary's definitions) or twitter like a bird, especially if the result of its use is a birdie.

Cleek – The old name for a 4-wood. A *Cleek* is also known as a thin or narrow bladed iron or putter.

Driver – A wood (a 1-wood) or a one iron.

Driving Cleek – A less lofted and probably longer shafted 4-wood used for driving.

Driving Iron – a 1-iron or any low lofted iron used to hit from the tee box.

Driving Mashie - 1 or 2-iron.

Hollow Iron - An Iron Head design that is made in two pieces. Rather bulbous in shape; the design concept is to move the CG away from the face to help get the ball airborne. Similar to smaller metal woods in that they are perimeter weighted.

Hybrid - Any one of a number of golf clubs that maintain characteristics of both a wood and an iron. Such clubs are often used in place of long irons in a player's set, for example the rescue club.

Jigger – A moderately lofted, shallow-faced, Hickory wood shafted iron club, usually the 4-iron.

Knife - Slang term applied to a #1 iron due to its lack of loft.

Lofter – The 6 or 8-iron.

Long Nose - The shape of a wooden club made in the 19th century. *Long Nose* clubs typically are longer than 4" when measured from heel to toe.

Mallet – A big wooden headed putter.

Mashie – Considered to be a 5-iron.

Mashie Niblick – A 7-iron.

Mid Iron – A 2-iron.

Mid Mashie – Is now a 3-iron.

Niblick – A 9-iron.

Pitching Wedge – A highly lofted iron, also called the 10-iron.

President – An iron having a steep loft equivalent to that of a Niblick, with a hole in the face, designed for playing out of water.

Rake - Also called the *Major Niblick*. It is a lofted iron having vertical slots through the face for playing out of water or sand. It was designed to reduce the interference of sand, or water between the ball and club face. A rake is also an item used to smooth sand traps after a golfer or a gopher has dug great holes in it.

Raylor - Fairway metal club of approximately 19 degrees of loft made popular by TaylorMade™.

Rescue Club - A generic name given to any number of clubs that combine features of a wood and an iron. Most "rescue" type clubs are designed to take the place of difficult-to-hit long irons. "Rescue" is also the trademark name of this type of club from TaylorMade™. This began the trend now called Hybrids.

Rut-Iron – (*Rutter, Track-Iron or Rutting Niblick*). A thin bladed iron used to hit out of ruts, divots etc.

Sammy – An iron similar to a *jigger*, but having a rounded back, used for approach shots.

Sand Wedge – A more lofted iron than a pitching wedge with a convex bottom for bouncing off the sand when getting out of traps or tall rough. Also used for shots like: chopping, chipping, poaching, punching, and pitching.

Schenectady - A putter with a big aluminum head.

Scraper – A lofted wooden club close to a 7-wood.

Spoon (Middle Spoon) – A 3-wood, less lofted than a *cleek*, to scoop the ball off the fairway or out of the light rough.

Spade Mashie – A 6-iron (more lofted than a *mashie* but less than a *lofter*).

Texas Wedge – The name for a putter when used from off the green.

Third Wedge – An iron that usually has the most loft and is a utility club used for short approach shots, high chip shots, and on occasions, pitching to slow or wet greens. It is normally this iron that convinces the golfer that the other two wedges he has are easier to hit. There are several types (52°, 54°, 56°, 58°, 60°, 62°, 64°), but the 60 degree *"L" or Lob wedge* is probably the most common.

Transitional - The size of a wooden-shafted club head, in-between the size of a *Bulger* and a *Long Nose* made in the late 1800's.

In about 1910, some deep grooved irons were introduced. Some with box grooves, waffle patterns, and corrugations, with names like *Deadstop, Stopem, Shur Shot, Holdem, and Bakspin.*

These clubs were remarkably effective at stopping the approach shots on the green. In fact, there were so efficient that after Jock Hutchison used one to win the 1912 British Open, the clubs were declared illegal.

In the 1930s, sand wedges were being offered with names like: *Scooper, Blaster, Sav-a-Shot, Sand Niblick, and Double-duty Niblick.*[17]

PARTS IS PARTS

Back-Weight – A piece of metal attached to the back of a wooden club head.

Blade – The class of irons identified by their equal weight distribution and a smooth back shape. Also known as a "muscle-back" iron due to a possible concentration of weight directly behind the center of the club face.

Butt Section – The larger end or grip end of the shaft.

Cavity Back – The design of a iron head in which the weight is distributed toward the perimeter of the head. Identified by; the recessed area on the back of the club head.

Face – The outlined or defined (and preferred) hitting surface of a golf club. There is a specific point on every club face called the *sweet spot*. It is difficult to say exactly where this spot is since every club is different but generally speaking, it is the dead center of the *bland belt* which is very near the *rotten region*, in the middle of the *lousy area* and surrounded by the *loathsome zone*. On wooden club heads the *sweet spot* is sometimes indicated by the heads of brass screws that are located on the face of the club head, hence the term *on-the-screws* is used when the ball is hit solid.

Ferrule – A tapered sleeve which forms a smooth transition from the top of the club's *hosel* to the shaft.

Grooves – The deep ruts (lines) on the club face. There are two distinct types, the sq*uare grooves* and the *standard V or U grooves*. Any grooves, no matter type, can not have a width greater than .035 inches or have a depth greater than .02 inches. In January 2010 the PGA changed the shape of the grooves to more a "V" and "U" shape with more rounded edges. This will cut down on the amount of spin a club can put on a golf ball.

Hosel – Also known as the neck is that portion of the wood or iron head that the shaft fits into or the *socket*.

Head – The head of a wood or iron club. The wood heads could be constructed of plastic, several different type of epoxy, metal, persimmon or laminated wood. Normally the iron head is a steel or a brass alloy.

Heel – The part of the club head nearest the hosel that rests on the ground at address.

Insert – A piece of material placed into the face of a wooden head, iron or putter.

Scoring – The groove design, logos, numbers, names, or any other writings etched into the sole plate or face of a wood head or the top, back, or side of any golf club.

Shaft – The steel, graphite, wood or other composite material portion of the club from the grip to the club head.

Sole – The bottom of a club head that would normally touch the ground when held by the grip.

Soleplate – The metal part attached to the bottom of wooden club heads.

Toe – The area of the club head that is the farthest from the shaft and hosel.

Whipping – The string wrapping which covers the neck or hosel of wooden clubs.

WHAT PARTS DO WHAT?

Bounce – Primarily found on sand wedges. It is when the trailing edge of the sole is lower than the leading edge in the square position. It helps the club to bounce off the ground or sand rather than to dig into it.

Bulge – The portion of the golfer that sticks out over his belt and past the ball position at address, also the horizontal curvature in degrees of the face of a wood club. The bulge of the club face helps to put spin on the ball.

Camper – Referred to as the rocker sole, radiused sole, or the 2-way and 4-way roll of the club. The radiused curve from toe to heel or leading edge or both, hence the 2-way or 4-way (the whole bottom of club).

Crown – The highest point at the top of a wooden club head.

Deep Face – Wooden clubs that have a face height of greater than about 2 inches.

Effective Loft – The loft of a wood when it is rolled into the square (0 degree) face angle position. Also the loft of a wooden club when the face and the shaft centerline are both perpendicular to the three dimensional target line. This gives the ball its highest or lowest trajectory.

Face Angle – The vertical angle of the face of a club in relation to the grounded sole line with the shaft perpendicular to the target line. Some clubs, especially putters, have face angles that are in a natural "closed" position (facing inward from the target line) or an "open" position (facing outward from the target line).

First Step – The first formed and defined visual transition to the increased diameter of a steal shaft. The distance between steps will help determine the "*kick point*" or "*flex-point*" of the shaft. See *shaft flex.*

Flange – A term that describes the elongation of the trailing (in some cases the leading) edge of an iron club or putter.

Hickory – Type of wood used make shafts for golf clubs. Some special made putters still have hickory wood for the shaft.

Hosel Offset – The distance from the front portion of the hosel to the front portion of the leading edge of the club head at the center of the face.

Lie - The angle between the shaft and the ground line when the club is measured in normal playing position resting on the crown of the sole.(see diagram on page 60)

Laminate – Layers of wood (usually maple) compressed and glued together and cut into blocks. From these blocks are shaped wooden club heads.

Loft - The angle created as measured from the club face in relation to a vertical line from the ground. The loft of a club will actually be determined by the relationship of the hosel position and/or the shaft position at ball impact.

Persimmon – A material with which to manufacture wooden heads. Made from a single block of wood and considered to be the best type of wooden woods.

Roll – The vertical curvature or radius measured from the crown to the sole on the face of a wooden club head. The roll of a club's face provides the correct spin or ball rotation to help the ball obtain the correct trajectory of flight after impact. A "toe" hit will cause the ball to start outward from the target line but curve back. A "heel" shot will cause the ball to start inward but again curve back.

Scoop – Also called *Dig*. On most clubs, the trailing edge of the sole or bottom of the club is higher off the ground than the leading edge. This allows the club head to "dig" into the ground rather than "*bounce*" off of it.

Shaft Bend Point – The point of maximum natural deflection during the bending of the shaft. Shafts are rated as to their flex points: Low flex (toward the club head and gives higher trajectory), Mid flex and High flex (toward the grip). Also called; the *kick-points*. The location of the maximum flex point on a shaft can be found immediately after the club is thrown or is used as a hammer.

Shaft Flex – A comparative measurement of a shaft's resistance to the bending or deflection of the shaft under a given amount of stress and load. Flexes are divided into the categories of:

> L (ladies – maximum flex)
> A (flexible – strong ladies, seniors, amateurs)
> R (medium flex)
> S (stiff)
> X (extra stiff)

Step Pattern – The order and lengths of the individual steps in a golf club's steel shaft which are used to indicate shaft model or brand and helps to determine flex point and amount of flex.

Swing Weight – A measurement which indicates the weight distribution of the club about a fixed fulcrum point of 14 inches. Expressed in letters (A to E) and numbers (0 to 9), such as C-9, D-2 or E–5, etc.

Temper – Metal transformation into a heated state in which stiffness and strength are imparted to steel shafts for golf clubs by the manufacture. Also, <u>mental</u> transformation into a heated state in which bends, crimps, and breaks are imparted to any type of shaft in golf clubs by the player.

CUSTOM GOLF CLUB FITTING PROGRAM

In early days, golfers were quite happy with just only one club (and often only one ball). It was about the end of the 15th Century that different clubs were crafted for special purposes and eventually iron clubs were added to the original wooden ones.

With the invention of the *Guttie* (a golf ball you will soon read about) and other rubber-cored balls also affected the design of the golf club. Lead and other materials were added to club heads to increase the weight. Inserts of various plastics, rubber, and graphite were added to woods, irons, and even putters to increase control. All of these innovative changes in conjunction with steel shafts and laminated wood heads facilitated the production of identical clubs and so the "Matched Set" was born.[3]

This lead to the manufacture of intermediate sizes and by the 1930's caddies were carrying around as many as 25 assorted clubs. It all became so ridiculous that the R & A and the USGA agreed to limit the number of clubs to 14, made up of woods, irons and a putter. So this then caused the player to be more versatile with fewer clubs and therefore requiring each club to be more matched to the others. I personally strictly adhere to the 18 club rule for you never know when you might need those extra wedges and hybrids! Of course I don't play in competition events anymore either.

The purpose of a custom fitting program is to provide the best possible matched set of clubs to an individual that results is a more consistent swing, better accuracy, and greater distance from hitting the ball with the sweet spot. Of course the swing is the most critical factor in custom fitting golf clubs. An individual's swing is first and foremost unique, therefore making the job of club fitting an experience that requires training and skill. *" The best wood in most amateur's bag is the pencil." www.com*

The primary reason that most people want to have custom fitted clubs is ego, but even then they do feel, as I do, that it helps improve their game. For those who really can't afford them, but want them anyway, I strongly believe that a set of matched clubs does help to play better golf. To play better golf though, takes more than just a good set of clubs. There are five basic steps to golf game improvement and they are:[18]

1. Professional swing instruction.
2. Properly fitted, quality equipment.
3. Practice, practice, practice.
4. Play, lots of it.
5. Positive attitude which includes capability to concentrate.

"An interesting thing about golf is, no matter how bad you are playing, it is possible to play worse." www.com

Note that the equipment, good or bad, is rated second. Even though a custom fitted set of clubs are an important step, it is not the most important. The most important step is the Professional Instruction (equipment use and mental control) for with that, any type of old, used, or new equipment could be adequate. Without instruction, the best and most expensive equipment, including a beautifully matched set of irons and woods, would be inadequate.

Golf is a game in which you fork over $800 for a set of clubs and then spend your weekend trying to use them as little as possible. [19]

THE TRUTH ABOUT LIES

OK! We have had our instructions and want to go to step 2 and get our new fitted clubs. Club fitting will adapt a set of clubs to your swing and will incorporate the following selections: Brand (Nike, Wilson, Ping, etc.) for looks and feel (I believe that if you don't like how the club looks you probably won't swing it well), type of club (forged or cast, blade or cavity back), type of shaft (steel or graphite), shaft length, flex and flex/kick point, grip type and size, club weight and swing weight, and the loft and lie of the club head. I am going to let your Professional Club Fitter provide all those answers but I am going to explain the importance of checking your clubs for "loft" and "lie" of the head. (See page 55 for the definition of *lie*)

When you receive your new clubs, the manufacturers do an excellent job of assembling them to fit the specifications provided by the fitter and your selections. But, in the areas of "*loft*" and "*lie*" they have neglected to provide adequate attention to and instead they just adapt the clubs to general standards that all the manufactures follow.

Most all manufacturers step the club head *lie* angle of the set of irons at about ½ of a degree per club. Example: a 6 iron with a 60 degree *lie* has its 5 iron with a 59 ½ degree *lie* and the 7 iron with a 60 ½ degree *lie*. I maintain that the steps or differences should be at least two thirds of a degree and adjusted up to 1° increments or greater.

I hope you find the following explanation interesting and consider having your clubs checked and readjusted for it does make a difference in how you strike the ball. If you don't like math especially trigonometry and algebra, you might want to skip the next few pages and not worry about the *lie* of your clubs or go directly to a good club repairman or proceed to page 64 and continue reading at Club Importance.

<u>LIES! LIES! LIES!</u>

The *lie* of the club during your swing is so very important to good shot making. If the *lie* is incorrect for your swing then the ball, when struck, could go off to the left or right depending whether the toe of the club is up too high or down too low. And, it is not how the club is assembled, but rather how it is adjusted to conform to your swing. This is where your club fitter and club repairmen come in. They should determine correct *lie* of the club for <u>your swing</u> while you are swinging the club (impact measurement) as well as taking the measurements at your address and stance (static measurement).

Most golfers do not maintain the same hand position established at address when making their swing. The hands will rise or move outward from the body during the swing as the body turns, causing the club head to tilt toe down. The difference between the two club head positions (static and impact position) must be adjusted for to allow a firm and flat contact with the ball during the swing.

The following is how I measure, calculate and adjust the club head to achieve the proper lie for custom clubs. First, I will consider the static measurement and develop a chart to represent the lie of each club at address.

We will be dealing with a right triangle (one angle being 90 degrees, refer to the diagram below). The three sides of the triangle are called the hypotenuse (the longest side opposite the right angle to be labeled side "c"), the adjacent side (the base line or side "b") and the opposite side (the side opposite of the acute or smaller angle labeled side "a").

Every right triangle has a consistent relationship or ratio between its 3 sides and two smaller angles. One relationship is between the sides and angles defined as the Trigonometry functions called the Sine and Cosine Functions of an angle (there are others but these is no need to go there).

The other relationship or ratio is between just the three sides and is called the Pythagorean Theorem whereas the square of the adjacent side (a^2) added to the square of the opposite side (b^2) will equal the square of the hypotenuse (c^2). Pythagorean Theorem is summarized as: $a^2 + b^2 = c^2$ or $a^2 = c^2 - b^2$

The Cosine function is: if the value of side "b" is divided by the value of side "c" the result is a decimal value representing the angle in degrees of the base angle which for our purposes is labeled the Angle of Lie (the angle between the shaft and the ground). The resulting decimal value from the division "b"/"c" can be converted to the value of the angle in degrees from a set of Trigonometry Tables.

Side "c" is the golf club length, side "b" is the vertical distance from the tip of the butt of the grip to the ground at address and during the swing, and side "a" is the distance from the grip butt vertical reference to the end of the golf club shaft.

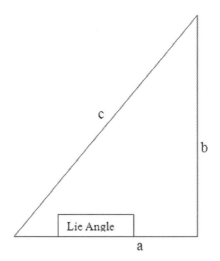

LIES PROVEN TRUE

As an example we will use a neutral standard 6 iron with a length of 37" with a 60° built in lie, which I have verified by measurement with a loft/lie gauge for static measurements and calculations. First we establish the values of "a" and "b" (since "c" is 37 inches in length) by getting the Cosine Function value from the trig tables for a 60 degree angle. That value is .8660. Since Cosine 60° = b/c or Cosine 60° times c = b, then .8660 times 37" = 32.04" the distance between the butt of the club and the ground. This value should remain constant throughout the computations for all the irons in a set assuming that the hand position at address should be at the same spot for each club. Only the *lie* angle changes as club length changes.

Since Pythagoras says that $a^2 = c^2 - b^2$ then $(a)^2 = (37)^2 - (32.04)^2$. Therefore $a^2 = 1369 - 1026.6$ or $a^2 = 342.4$ Taking the square root of both sides: a = 18.5" the ground distance from the bottom of the hosel to the bottom of side b. This value will change one inch for every ½ inch change in club length.(side "c") "c" = 37 ½ ", "a" changes to 19.5" considering that side "b" remains constant. <u>This results in a change of the lie angle and ball impact results.</u>

Sine Function of the lie angle = a/c or 19.5" divided 37 ½" for a 5 iron, equals .5195 which represents a 58.6° lie angle. So by changing from a 6 to a 5 iron the *lie* angle changed 1.4° and not the 1/2° of change as recommended by the manufacture's standards. The following table indicates how the length of the irons change effects the lie angle and by what degree according to the calculations above.

Iron	Club Length	Side "a" Length	Side "b" Length	Lie Angle	Variance to next club
3	38.5"	21.5"	32.04"	56.3°	+ 1.2°
4	38"	20.5"	32.04"	57.5°	+ 1.1°
5	37.5"	19.5"	32.04"	58.6°	+ 1.4°
6	37"	18.5"	32.04"	60°	+ 1.3°
7	36.5"	17.5"	32.04"	61.3°	+ 1.7°
8	36"	16.5"	32.04"	63°	+ 1.5°
9	35.5"	15.5"	32.04"	64.5°	+ 1.8°
PW	35"	14.5"	32.04"	66.3°	+ 1.8°

This data indicates that the progressive change of the *lie* of a club that is ½" longer is greater than 1° twice the 1/2° the manufactures suggest. This data reflects exact dimensions and does not compensate for error in measurements and differences that a player may introduce by varying address postures hence static and impact hand position measurements. Considering these factors the small changes in player stance and swings will cause an immeasurable tolerance during fitting sessions. Therefore allowing for up to a 20% tolerance in the measurements the *lie* angle would still differ from club to club by at least 1° plus or minus .2° satisfactory for most playing conditions.

Now let us consider an example of changing the hand's position (grip butt position in relation to the ground, side "b") during an impact swing when the hands are moved out 1" and up 2/3" and see how the data in the chart above varies with these new values. For every inch outward movement side "a" decreases 1 inch. The outward movement of the hands will also cause side "b" to change 2/3 since the hands have moved up to keep the correct distance to the ball since "c" remains constant. The following chart indicates what the lie angles should be for the iron set during a swing to maintain a correct ball impact. Only a few clubs are listed to show the dramatic changes that take place during a swing. I left a calculation for you to check if you are so inclined.

Iron	ClubSide Length	"a"Side Length	"b"Side Length	Lie Angle	Variance to 1st chart
3	38.5"	20.5"	32.7"	58.3°	+ 2°
4	38"	19.5	32.7"	59.2°	+ 1.7°
5	37.5"	18.5"	32.7"	60.8°	+ 2.2°
6	37"	17.5"	32.7"		

Using the same tolerances listed above, the small movement of the hands from the "static" position to the new "impact" position causes the *lie* of the club to change 2° plus or minus .4° This amount of change does not take in account the added amount of *lie* change due to the shaft bending during the swing due to gravity and downward inertia which would increase the amount of variance to an even 2° change from static to impact club head *lie* angle corresponding to an inch of outward hand movement.

All this is not a lie. Check your own clubs and plug in the values in the formulas above to see what condition your clubs are in.

BACKWARDS LOFT

I would be remiss if I didn't stress the second aspect of your new set of clubs that will help or hinder you from scoring better. This of course is the *loft* of a club which will determine two things: How high the ball will go after impact and how much distance the ball will carry. Distance is the more critical aspect of *loft* and therefore I will only mention a few things that I think important in having the correct *loft* deviations from one iron to the next. By the way, height if the ball flight is important, especially when closer to the green, because the ball will stop closer to initial landing area with steeper decent angles.

When new clubs are delivered, the *loft* progressive pattern or degree step between clubs is normally in 3° increments or 4°s or a mixed 3° to 4° increments. For example your clubs could be one of these:

3° Step		4° Step		3° to 4° Step	
Iron	Loft	Iron	Loft	Iron	Loft
3	22	3	22	3	22
4	25	4	26	4	26
5	28	5	30	5	28
6	31	6	34	6	32
7	34	7	38	7	36
8	37	8	42	8	40
9	40	9	46	9	44
PW	43	PW	50	PW	48

You can see that between the different stepping patterns of the sets change dramatically toward the loftier irons. Also note that the smaller steps are at the beginning of the chart or between the longer irons. Now the distance that the *loft* allows per club seems to be shorter between the smaller numbered irons and widens as the iron increase in *loft*. The more *loft* differences between clubs, the more distance variance between clubs.

If, for example, 1° of loft equals about 3 – 4 yards of distance for a particular swing, the distance that the 3 iron carries over the 4 iron would be (see table on page 63): Column 1 & 3 = 9 to 12 yards, Column 2 = 12 to 16 yards. Now consider the 9 iron and the PW in all Columns the distance between irons would be 12 to 16 yards. Now these distance values seems to me to be backwards. Wouldn't you rather have the larger distance differences at the opposite end of the Columns? I would! Let me explain.

I think they are backwards because: at greater distances from the green, the distance between irons is not that critical. You are trying to hit a target that is, on the average, about 20 to 40 yards in size (average green). You have a target that could be hit with either of two clubs, the 3 or 4 or maybe the 4 or 5. So the loft of these clubs could be separated by a greater number of degrees (column 2).

Now consider when you are closer to the green and your target area is much smaller and the distance to the target is more critical. You do want to hit as close to the pin as possible don't you? Well then your clubs with greater *loft* progressions can't give you the narrower choice of distances when they are separated by distances of 12 – 15 yards (4 degrees between club lofts). It makes more since that if your 9 iron and wedges are only separated by 2 degrees (hence distance between clubs is now 6 to 8 yards) you could be more precise in club selection and put the ball to a more precise distance and be closer to the pin using a consistent swing.

Here is my perception of how clubs should be lofted:

Iron	Loft	Iron	Loft	Iron	Loft	Iron	Loft
3	29	6	43	9	52	UW	56
4	35	7	46	PW	54	LW	58
5	39	8	49	SW	55 10^0 bounce		

The variation from the PW and SW is only one degree because of the bounce difference of the SW which would not be used in the fairway normally whereas the Utility Wedge would be used in its place and is only 2 degrees from the Pitching Wedge maintaining a proper *loft* progression for the more "distance accurate" shots closer to the green.

CLUB IMPORTANCE

The three most important golf clubs are considered to be: The Driver, Putter, and the Wedge. Psychologically, the Drive is very important because if you hit your tee shot well, it fills you with confidence. On the other hand, if you smash a couple of drives into the woods, your confidence can be shaken.[20]

What is more important is knocking putts into the cup. A good putter is a match for anyone; a bad putter is a match for no one.[18] The woods are literally full of long hitting drivers but remember that 47 to 50% of all golf is putting (figuring that par is normally 72 for 18 holes, this is considering that it will normally take two putts on every hole, hence 50% of the score).

Let us not forget the wedge. This instrument in the hand of a master can shave off a lot of strokes from one's game. It is a very versatile club used in most every situation around the green that you can think of and even a few you can't even imagine. It is probably the only club that requires you to make a multitude of different swings sometimes due to the loft differences between the different wedges in your set of irons. Ah, but when do you use this club? It is normally when you miss an approach shot to the green, note above where it says "every situation <u>around </u>the green". If you are using a wedge for anything but an approach shot, it definitely could be the most important club because you have to use it well especially if you can't putt.

The arguments go on, and on, and on..... Which club then is the most important to you and which do you practice with the most? Which club do you play the best? Which one do you play the worst? Do you lose more shots off the tee, off the fairway or on the green? You should practice the shot that gives you the most trouble, how else can you become more proficient at it??? Or you could ask a professional how to correct it, but of course there goes your excuses for playing bad.

You really should practice the shots that give you the most trouble, and then double that amount of time with the putter on the practice green. You could of course always ask your 18 handicap playing partner "What am I doing wrong?" He and everyone else, is fully qualified to tell you what your doing wrong, but see a teaching professional when you want to ask "What can I do to correct it?"

SPECIALIZED CLUBS

Long shafted clubs

There are three basic contributing factors involved in golf club specifications that determine a club's capability to increase shot distance. They are weight (center of gravity), shaft length and club face loft. If the weight of the club head is increased and the speed of the head is held constant, distance will increase. When the weight of the club head is held constant but the speed of the club head is increased, distance will also increase but at a greater amount.

This has to do with Kinetic energy, the form of energy associated with the speed of an object. Its equation is: $KE = \frac{1}{2} mv^2$, or stated simply that kinetic energy is equal to ½ the mass times the velocity squared. Now isn't that simple? Now don't panic we are not getting into math again! But, it should be obvious to the most casual observer that increasing club head speed has more potential for producing more distance than increasing the club head weight.[3] Now for those of you who don't give a squat about all that, just swing your big Bertha harder and faster and the ball will go further.

As an illustration that weight is not the answer I provide the following from the book "Search for the Perfect Swing: "if a driver is swung at 100 mph, and had a head of 14 oz, twice the normal weight , (it) would send the ball away is at 149 mph. A highly heavy one of 16 oz would push the speed up only to 165 mph. Even one weighing 10,000 tons traveling at the same 100 mph would only send the ball away at 166 mph."

Question then is: Should the speed of the club head be increased with shaft length? Or should it be done by decreasing the weight of the club head? The answer depends on the individual golf swing of the player. A lighter club may not change the club head speed because the hand speed that is swinging the club may not change no matter how light the club may be. It seems logical, that if a person's swing can be held constant, then by lengthening the shaft of the club it should give the club head a greater speed at impact, hence more distance.

"The average golfer who swings a 43-inch driver at a club head speed of 120 feet per second in the hitting area can attain a club head speed of 123.5 feet per second with a 44-inch driver, providing he can swing it at the same hand speed". Sam Snead[20] *"Swing easy, hit hard."*

The trick of getting more distance with increased shaft length is swing the club with the same hand speed. The means developing a swing that consistently produces solid hits (impacts on the center of gravity) while maintaining a consistent hand speed (swing stability and tempo). In this case, the longer shafted clubs will produce increased distance.

Both solutions above deal with the equipment being used while keeping the swing consistent. Other methods of increasing distance are addressing the swing such as increasing rotation and hand speed. More rotation and faster rotation increases club head speed. One other item that could be changed to increase distance is the hands and use of the wrists during the golf swing. The wrists are naturally cocked during the club take away but changing the point where the wrists are un-cocked can help increase club head speed and increase distance.

Once you have increased your distance, maintaining it requires you to be consistence in impacting the ball in the center of the club face, the "sweet spot." An off center impact will cause you to lose distance. Off center hits of about one half a inch will cause a loss of about 7% , of the average, of your normal distance. A off center hit of one inch could be a loss of between 15 and 17% of your normal distance. A normal 300 yard drive could be shortened to only about 250 yards with a one inch off center impact. So keeping your distance consistent will require: a consistency of your swing that will give you more "sweet spot" hits and maybe that added distance you wanted in the first place.

> *"Art said he wanted to get more distance. I told him to hit it and run backwards."* Ken Venturi on Art Rosenbaum.

For the amateur or high handicapper, this consistency could be attained by using the newer square headed drivers where the head weight is moved from the center outward toward the heel and the toe of the club head. They do help you keep your distance during off center hits but not 100%.

Graphite Shafted clubs

There are three good reasons why graphite shafts would be used instead of the conventional steel shafts. The first is the overall weight of the club is reduced. Second, the graphite shaft will buffet (reduce the shock) the impact stress places on the arms and elbows when hitting the ground and ball. Third, graphite is more flexible which helps to increase club head speed, hence more distance. The down side of switching to graphite shafts is that you will probably over swing the club and lose some control in trade for the added distance. Have your swing analyzed by a professional when switching to new equipment.

Long Shafted Putters

The use of the long shafted putters is an option that is as individual as the putting grip and putting stroke. It is a matter of choice and is no better or no worse than the normal length putter shafts. The best way to determine if long shaft is good for you or not, is to try one for yourself. If you are having so much trouble that you have to change to a longer putter shaft, go see a professional instructor for help with your putting. It may or may not be the equipment you're using it may just be in <u>how</u> you are using it.

Remember the book I recommended reading back on page 2. It contains a great chapter on putting with long shafted putters, why and how.

An old adage: *"The best way to putt is the way you putt best."*[4]

CHAPTER VI

"Dimples"

THE GOLF BALL

The golf ball too, has a history. The first mention is of a feather-stuffed ball in 1620 called the "*featherie*". Because of the nature of their construction (all were hand stitched), golf balls were more often oval-shaped than round, which affected the way they behaved. Rarely were they consistent in size or weight and were fragile and tended to break apart when struck by a heavy headed iron club.

Golf balls were also made of wood, carved into a round shape. In the 1700's the golf balls began to be made in the town of St Andrews, Scotland with leather covers stuffed with a top hat full of goose feathers. Each ball took one man approximately three hours to make and three seconds to lose.[21]

When the properties of gutta-percha (obtained from rubber latex trees) were discovered in about 1846 or 1848, golf ball manufacturing became simpler and the balls (called *Gutty* or *Gutties*) were truly spherical. Experience proved that this ball flew farther and straighter if scarred (this was the precursor to golf ball dimples as we know them today). Gutta Percha balls would lose shape though, after a couple of rounds, requiring it to be reheated and remolded. Besides losing their shape other variance was weight. They were made in a range of weights each golfer choosing which he thought was the best for him or for the conditions at the time. The *gutty* was more durable and performed better than the *featherie*, and because it was much harder, it had a tendency to chip and crack clubheads.

In about 1898, Coburn Haskell invented the rubber wound ball, aided by John Gammetter of B.F Goodrich Co. who developed the ball winding machine, which remains little changed from his original design. The Haskill patent defined a liquid center or solid core, wound with rubber thread under high tension and covered with molded gutta percha or balata rubber.[21]

The next step was the introduction of the rubber-core ball, which offered not only better performance but also made playing easier for beginners. This ball too, came in a range of weights, but in 1921 the R & A and the USGA got together and agreed on a standard weight. Over the years to follow, factors were modified, but balls are now being standardized at 46g (1.68 ounces), with a diameter of 43 cm (1.68 inches). The smaller European 4.2 cm (1.62 inch) diameter ball has gradually been phased out.

About the turn of the century, 1900, ATTI Engineering of New Jersey began making ball molds. For decades, most balls used the ATTI dimple pattern of concentric circles. Current physics and computers confirm ATTI's findings, that dimples should cover from 25 to 75 percent of the ball's surface with dimples from .09 to .15 inches in diameter, with a depth of no more than 1/8 the diameter of the dimple.[21]

The pre-dominate pattern of dimples prior to the 1970's was the *Octohedral* or *Attihedral* pattern. This dimple pattern comprised of four straight rows of dimples around the middle of the ball, with four around each pole. Small triangular arrays of dimples fill the remaining area on the ball. This creates 8 triangular groupings of dimples on the ball.

In the early 1970's the *Icosahedral* dimple pattern was introduced and is the most popular pattern in use today. The pattern arranges the dimples into 20 triangular groups, allowing the same air pressure on all parts of the ball as it flies through the air, reducing wind resistance.

Other patterns were also developed and used different size dimple diameters and groupings such as the *Tetrahedral,* a dimple pattern that consisted of four large triangles.

In 1966, James Bartsch with Princeton Chemical Research developed the first solid core ball, later called the PCR Bartsch.[21]

In 1973 a chemist with Spalding, Robert Molitor developed the SYRLYN cover.[21]

The introduction of the GUTTY and then the rubber-cored and rubber-wound ball also affected the design of the golf club.

The 1980's saw a plethora (alright, so I found a new word and used it. It means overabundance or excess, but of course everyone but me knew that already) of new materials and various dimple patterns and numbers (examples 374, 392, 444, 492, etc., depict the number of dimples or the type of dimple pattern used), sizes, colors, and compressions (80, 90 and 100). They are made from *Balata, Lithium Balata, Surlyn, Lithium Surlyn, Zinthane, Lotek, Zylin* and now Titleist has introduced a new *Elastomer* covered ball and Wilson Staff the *Ionomer*. Some are made for more distance, some for more control, and some for more back spin or ball stopping capabilities.

Choosing the right ball to play with will depend on several factors: time of year (in winter or cold weather a lower compression ball is desirable), barometric altitude of the golf course (balls travel farther in Colorado than in Florida), air density (humidity), wind conditions, and other situations such as: rain, snow, hot and dry weather, or even if you are playing in the morning or after noon. Other factors are the course to be played, is it a long course or a short to medium course, does it have big or small greens, are the green soft or hard, do they putt fast or slow. The choice of compression, dimple pattern, color and manufacture is really a personal preference and should be based on club head speed as well as swing capabilities, likes and dislikes.

Of course there are other factors that help us to decide which ball to use such as: how much did it cost (anything for a dollar or less is acceptable), how old was it when I found it, where did I find it (water logged balls tend to lose performance), how many cuts, scrapes, or scratches does it have, and the most important reason for choosing a particular ball to play is......... is the next shot over water*???* *"When your shot has to carry over a water hazard, you can either hit one more club or two more balls." www.com*

Current annual worldwide golf ball production exceeds 250,000,000 +. No wonder I have a hard time deciding on which ball to use, especially when I'm hitting over water..... *"Why is it that it is twice as difficult to hit a ball over water than sand?" www.com*

IS THERE A BETTER NAME FOR THE GOLF BALL THAN "DIMPLES?"

Ball – A small round object that comes in odd colors covered with dimples and an occasional smile. They can be bought in stores, golf shops, or from small children. The can be found in water hazards, wooded areas on the golf course, deep rough, and on occasions in the fairways of any golf course.

Ball Deemed to Move – A ball is deemed to have moved if it leaves its position and comes to rest in any other place. A ball has not moved if it only jiggles or oscillates.[8]

Ball Holed Out – A ball is *holed* when it lies within the circumference of the hole and all of it is below the level of the lip or edge of the hole.[8]

Ball-in-Play - A ball is *in-play* as soon as the player has made a stroke on the teeing ground. It remains *in-play* until holed-out, except when it is out-of-bounds, lost or lifted, or another ball has been substituted under applicable rule.[8]

Buried-Lie – When more than half of the ball is in or under sand or mud or deep grass. Yes, I said on page 2 that we wouldn't go there but this is golf so you should be prepared to expect the unexpected.

Check-up – When a ball is hit to the green and it stops on the second bounce like it had brakes.

Dimple-Pattern - Golf balls will have indentations of different or varying sizes and arranged in a multitude of patterns depending on the manufacture.

Experienced Golf Balls – Golf balls that you lost either out-of-bounds, in water hazards, or in the deep rough that are found or retrieved by local kids or the Pro-shop that you can buy back at a reduced price.

Feathery – A kind of golf ball made with goose feathers.

Flier – A ball that has reduced backspin and therefore can travel farther than normal. This is caused when hitting from the rough and grass or any other element gets between the club head and the ball, preventing the club head's grooves to come in contact with the ball at impact.

Floater – A ball struck from deep grass which comes out and travels shorter than normal due to heavy cushioning of the blow from a plethora (there's that word again) of grass between the ball and the club face. It is also a golf ball that will float in water.

Four Piece Ball – A golf ball constructed from four specific materials. There will be a central core surrounded by windings covered by a harder secondary cover (for distance) and a softer outer cover (for spin and feel).

Gutta-Percha – A solid ball made from gutta percha packing rubber.

Guttie – A rubber based golf ball used before the 20th century about 1848 to 1898.

Legs – A ball is said to have *legs* if it continues to roll a significant distance after landing. If it bounces into the rough and becomes wedged under a rock or in a crook of a tree, it is said to have *claws*. If it runs down a bank and into a water hazard, it has *fins*. If on a putt, it rings the cup without going in the hole, it has *lips*. If it takes a good bounce and rolls toward the hole, it has *eyes*. If the ball reacts to verbal commands, it has *ears*. If it is hit with the bottom edge of an iron and cut, it is said to have a *smile*. And, if it does all the wrong things on any hole, it is given *wings* and flung into the nearest water hazard or thick underbrush where it becomes an *experienced ball*.

Liquid Center – Term generically given to three-piece balls as most have a center core of a liquid.

Lost Ball – A ball is lost if:

> It cannot be not found, or cannot be identified as his by the player within 5 minutes after the player's *side* or his or their *caddies* have begun to search for it; or
> The player has made a *stroke* at a *substitute* ball; or
> The player has made a *stroke* at a *provisional ball* from the place where the original ball is likely to be or from a point neared the hole than that place.[8]
> Advice from actor/comedian Leslie Nelson: "*Never pick up a lost ball while it is still moving.*"

Membership Bounce – When the ball takes a better than expected bounce when badly hit or hit off target line and usually away from trouble and towards the hole.

Mesh - Type of turn-of-the-century ball made from gutta-percha characterized by a pattern of intersecting lines on the cover.

Pop-Fly – When the ball is hit with the top edge of the club face and it goes straight up.

Putty – An old golf ball that was softer than a *guttie* used for putting.

Provisional Ball – A ball played under Rule 27-2 for a ball which may be *lost* outside a *water hazard* or may be out-of-bounds. It ceases to be a provisional ball when rules provide that the player continue play with it as the *ball-in-play* or that it be abandoned.[8]

Spherical Symmetry – USGA rule parameter that states: regardless of how a ball is positioned at address or struck at impact, the ball must perform the same in respect to ball flight versus ball orientation.[8]

Spin – The rotation of a ball induced by the club face causing the ball to hook, slice or *spin-back* on the green. *High Spin* – Any of a number of golf balls designed for maximum spin and control. Generally soft feeling and preferred by better players. *Low Spin* – Any of a variety of golf balls designed for less spin. Generally harder and yields more distance.

Spin Rate – The amount of spin on a golf ball. A *High Spin* ball will carry higher and longer and roll less than a *Low Spin* ball that flies lower and rolls more for greater distance. *High Spin* balls will react better to side spin hence are said to be easier to draw or fade.

Solid Ball – Also known as a *Two-Piece* ball, a solid ball is characterized as one with a cover molded over a central core. *Solid balls* are considered to have a harder feel and may tend to go farther than other types of balls.

Stony (Stiff) – A shot to the green where the ball is close to the hole.

Stymie – When an object is directly in line with the desired trajectory of the ball.

Substitute Ball – A ball put into play for the original ball that was either in *play, lost, out of bounds* or lifted.

Three Piece - A generic term given to a ball with a center core, rubber windings and a cover. It may also have a center (some of steel) and two "cover" materials, eliminating the windings.

Two Piece – A type of ball characterized by a center core surrounded by a cover made of a durable material.

Unplayable – When a ball is marked, cut, or out-of-round, it is deemed to be unsuitable for continued play and cannot be used.

Wrong Ball – It is any ball other than the ball-in-play or a provisional ball or, in stroke play, a second ball played under rule 3-3 or rule 20-7c.[8]

Jack Lemmon: *"If you think it's hard to meet new people, try picking up the wrong golf ball."*

THE GOLF GLOVE

When the great golf-history books are finally written, the golf glove might merit a paragraph, maybe just a caption. Golf gloves are not named like putters, they are not coddled like hand crafted persimmon drivers, and most pros use at least one new glove for each round, tossing the used piece of leather away like, well like a used piece of leather. A glove is a forgettable, disposable, and only slightly more fascinating than say, a white tee.

Gloves, for all their current high-tech, water-repellent qualities, are not a relatively new commodity. They have been around golf since before the turn of the 20th century and some have suggested that original LPGA card-holder Mary Queen of Scots was a glove wearer back when she was teeing it up in the 16th century.

In the first half of the 20th Century, gloves were hardly the near necessity they have become today. They were, when they appeared, at best an adornment, and most often, an oddity. Not much, therefore, was happening to the golf glove up to the late 1930's, until Henry Cotton won the British Open in 1937 at a rain soaked Carnoustie course, maintaining his grip with a gloved left hand. Good players began to take notice. As a result of Cotton's instructions on golf being 85 percent hands, he recommended a glove to protect the swing's most valuable tool and control, the left hand.

But what was the beginning? Where did Henry get his glove? Maybe.... once upon a time, as the fables begin (though it was more likely in the late 1920's), a venerable wealthy Scot was golfing at Gleneagles. He was formidable off the tee, but also egregiously wild, due mainly to his chronic inability to maintain a firm grip on the club. At last, one drive flew over a clump of trees and buried itself deep in the heather, but the gentleman, cut from the archetypal Scottish mold, tramped in after it. He lost sight of his foursome, but kept up the search, all the while musing over the problem of his unsure grip. Suddenly, he came upon, of all things, a young farm lass sitting placidly in the midst of a clearing and milking her cow. On her left hand, she wore (most strange) a glove, and in answer to the obvious question, she told the Scot, "It helps my grip." In a heat of inspiration, he purchased it from her on the spot and ran back to show his companions. From that day forth, he was never without a glove, and he played happily ever after. The golf glove was born.

Natives of Gleneagles swear that this apocryphal story is true, and indeed it may be. If so, it is a contemporary of a similar American account of the discovery of the golf glove, a story only slightly more prosaic. H.G. Hilts & Co. were the manufactures of the first commercial golf glove, and it was probably Harry Hilts who made the original fortuitous discovery. Hilts rarely played golf but was lured into a game one day by a prospective customer. Surprisingly, the threesome also included one E.G. Willard, Hilt's biggest competitor for the guest's business. Hilts, did not even own a set of clubs, was playing poorly and being baited by both his customer and the leering Willard. Finally, Willard challenged Hilts to a bet, wagering that he could out-drive him on the seventh hole. Wet and cold from the steady drizzle that had been falling since play began, Hilts by now was enraged. He rushed to the next tee and, without stopping to remove the pale gray dress gloves he was wearing, drove ferociously into the mist. It was the longest drive of his life, and he won the bet easily.

The first glove produced by the company was called the Hilts Golf Palm. Made of thick leather, the palm was not really a glove at all: it had no fingers and covered only the center of the hand. In the 1930's, Don Willard (the son of E.G.) designed the short fingered glove, which was simply a regular man's glove with the fingers cut short. The development then progressed to the open-backed design and by the mid 1930's it became the full-fingered glove as we know it today.[15]

"There are two things you can learn by stopping your backswing at the top and checking the position of your hands: how many hands you have, and which one is wearing the glove." www.com

CHAPTER VII

"Are Lessons Really Necessary?"

ABOUT GOLF LESSONS [22]

"The player who expects a lesson to 'take' without subsequent practice just isn't being honest with himself or fair to his professional." Gary Player [4]

Golf lessons, in themselves, do not make you a better golfer and they are not supposed to take the place of practice, but rather to enhance practice and make it worthwhile. When practicing and incorporating the information gained in golf lessons, attainable goals should be established before practice so that positive results can be seen. By setting the goals before practice you will know when you have reached a particular goal then you can move on to the next or be ready for additional instruction.

Golf should really to be learned starting from the hole (or cup on the putting surface) progressing backwards to the tee box. First thing to learn is the feel of the ball off the putter and into the hole. This is where golf lessons should start. It is where learning begins, the feel of striking a ball at short distances. It is also the beginning of learning a golf swing. A youngster or beginning golfer should practice around the putting green, then progress to the side of the green with a pitching wedge or some kind of a chipping iron, then move out to the approach area with longer irons and finally to the tee box.

The chipping or pitching stroke is just a small version of a full golf swing. All other shots are an extension of that basic swing. But, that swing is not much good without the touch or feel of the ball, and to get that, it takes lots of practice on and around the practice putting green. Because the golf swing is still small at this point of instruction, tempo, mental and physical discipline, and thought control is easier to teach and establish.

LOW HANDICAPPERS

For the experienced golfer, lessons are to correct inherited bad habits, those already acquired or those being acquired. The older we get, our golf swing and playing abilities will change. Our physical capabilities change with age, disease, and even the food we eat affect our daily strength and energy levels. Lessons will help achieve a good transition from one swing to another or getting back to the old swing. It is almost impossible to see changes in ourselves and our swing, therefore, it may require a trained professional with a keen eye, good communication skills, an excellent knowledge of the mechanics of golf, and the ability to change the minimum amount of a golf swing as possible to get desired results.

BEGINNERS

For the beginning golfer, lessons are essential, especially from a qualified instructor, and practice is most important for learning to swing a golf club well enough to move to the course for actual play. If the instructor cannot perform what he teaches (visual feedback is an important key to learning), find another instructor. Beginners should be taken through the process of learning golf in several slow but progressive steps, each being completed before attempting to play any course. I believe that the first steps of learning to play good golf are: proper grip, a balanced stance at address, and establishing a good steady tempo during every swing. Next are progressive steps starting with short putts, medium putts and then long putts, short chips etc, etc, etc. The last step is using woods. Most first year golf classes provided at any college or university are very adequate for the beginner golfer.

ALL GOLFERS

Additional reasons for taking lessons are to learn more about the game and raise your level of play. Of course without practice, all the knowledge in the world about golf will not help you score better. Lessons also can help a player manage his or her swing on the course or under various playing conditions. Many times, lessons will help build confidence and when used in practice can result in a reduction of strokes during play.

THE TEACHING PROFESSIONAL

"Golf is the most over taught and least learned human endeavor. If they taught sex the way they teach golf, the race would have died out years ago." Jim Murray, Sports Columnist.[11]

I can't speak for other teaching professionals, but I think the ability to teach is a gift that I have developed, trained for, and used for over 46 years. Most of which was teaching in a formal classroom environment. But for 20+ years I have been teaching golf, giving lessons (sixteen years as a swing analyst and two as a touring professional player) and generally educating golfers about the game of golf and about the mechanics of their individual golf swing.

"I have always thought that the best golf teachers are those who have played professionally or have had a great deal of competitive experience. They know which swings and techniques will work under pressure, because they have used them in pressure situations." J.C. Snead[23]

With several exceptions, golf professionals and pro golfers should not consider PGA certification the keystone to good teaching. Some of the PGA golf professionals are not very good communicators, and yet many golfers who haven't even finished business school can push players to varying levels of success. *"If a teacher ever tells you there is only one way to play, he's not the best."* Gary Player[4]

According to Chris Hunkler, the PGA senior director of membership programs, *"To teach – and to teach correctly – is the cornerstone of the professional. Good teaching is based on good communication. If a professional takes time to wander up and down the range, he can make quick pointers and chat with the players informally. It gives them a feeling he cares about their games, and they'll be more likely to come see him on a more formal basis for help with their games."* Hunkler, like any good teacher, stresses communication as the key to worthwhile instruction. It doesn't matter how much information you have at your disposal if you can't transfer that information to your student effectively through sound communication, it is worthless. Communication includes action as well as word exchanges that is why an instructor should be able to perform what he teaches.

Larry Miller, author of a golf instruction book called Holographic Golf understands the role of the professional as a teacher, and while he doesn't think his peers are misinformed about the golf swing, he sees a crisis in the application of what they do know.

According to Larry Miller, "*There are as many ways to swing as there are people playing, and an instructor must find a way to help them make the most of their swing. What good instruction does, is impart the fundamentals within the parameters of a successful swing – that's the heart of the argument.*"

Will Lampley, who wrote Swing Dynamics – How to Teach The Modern Golf Swing says, "*Golf is a simple game that is made difficult by the way it is taught and the way it is practiced. For a player to improve and realize his potential, he needs competent, consistent instruction, regular practice, and solid equipment.*"

"*One of the biggest reasons we can't always translate the words of our instructors into effective swings is we really don't understand what our instructor is saying.*" Joseph C Dey[4]

A good teacher communicates effectively to build a sound, repeatable golf swing though sound application of a sound principle. A player's level of performance is the product of natural abilities, but it can be developed through swing knowledge and instruction. A good teacher will be a coach that reaffirms his confidence in the player and gets confidence back when they see the student's game improve.[24]

To improve your game through professional instruction, find a teaching professional that will work with your swing to improve your abilities through sound principles, not text book teaching that tries to make everyone swing the same. Your swing is unique and is effective according to your abilities and talents. Find someone who can communicate to you instruction that develops those abilities and talents to increase your swing knowledge.

Harvey Penick on the sexes: "*No pretty woman can miss a single shot without a man giving her some poor advice. A husband should never try to teach his wife to play golf or drive a car. A wife should never try to teach her husband to play bridge.*"[20]

I have quoted a lot of good golf teachers and do agree with what they say about instruction and communication. But, I have noticed that there is very little mentioned about the thought process (concentration) a player goes through while performing a swing. Here is the area that better golf can have its beginning. A most important step to becoming better at most anything is to control your concentration during the time being used to accomplish an objective (golf swing).

A good golf instructor, that spends time helping you learn how to concentrate and develop your thinking processes and concentration levels, can raise your level of play more than any instructor that leans only on the physical aspects of the swing. He must address attitudes, swing thoughts, specific concentration points and an over-all understanding how your mind controls your swing and abilities.

Raise your concentration level and lower your score. The first step and the hardest thing to do, is to quit thinking about hitting a ball and instead concentrate on just swinging a club. Whether it is a specific spot you want to hit to, or a direction or a multitude of other thoughts, your mind is usually on the wrong thing at the wrong time just prior to a bad shot. Good golf requires a high level of concentration skills. But, realize that "Real Golf" requirements are not so restrictive to just having fun playing golf. The definition of "Real Golf" is explained in Chapter X.

Review page xv for the notes from Chuck Hogan and myself to you about what the game of golf is. That's what you should be concentrating on. Keep reading. Chapter X will help.

CHAPTER VIII

"Here, Hold It This Way!"

THE GRIP

"Most people don't realize it, but the primary difference between a good golfer and a bad one lies in the grip." Julius Boros[4]

"The basic factor in all good golf is the grip. Get it right and all other progress follows." Tommy Armour[4]

"It is impossible to play good golf without a proper grip." Sam Snead [4]

"A correct grip is a fundamental necessity in the golf swing." Bobby Jones[4]

The grip is the foundation of a swing. Remember, that the grip is your only connection with the club and hence the ball. *"The grip is the crucial junction point which all the body's strength and rhythm are transmitted to the club."* Arnold Palmer[4]

If you have a bad grip, you don't want a good swing (a quote from Ben Hogan). With a bad grip you have to make unattractive adjustments in your swing to hit the ball squarely. *"Without a proper grip no player can expect to hit accurate shots with even a fair degree of consistency."* Gary Player[4]

As an experienced golf instructor and from reading everything I can on "Teaching Golf" including quotes and thoughts of some of the greatest players, I have learned that the player's grip is a delicate but the most important matter that needs to be addressed especially at the beginning of any instruction. Changing a bad grip into a better grip requires a great amount of practice and the student must be willing to do it. The instructor must be willing and able to <u>explain</u> and <u>demonstrate</u> the reason for the grip change to validate all the work it will take on the student's part to change. I have observed many golf instructors teaching a student how to swing a club but never addressing the student's bad grip. This is the most critical element of playing golf that a beginner must understand and accept. "*The grip is the most important single consideration in learning to play winning golf.*" Byron Nelson[4]

It is important to check the grip at the last minute, if the hands are on the club correctly leave them alone. If the hands are moved anytime prior to the swing completion, they camouflage a poor grip and will probably get calluses or blisters and have a lot of approach shots to the green from deep trouble. "*Unless a player gets his or her grip correct, trouble begins immediately.*" Bobby Locke[4]

TYPES OF GRIPS

There are three types of grips used consistently today. A popular grip called the VARDON or OVERLAPPING grip is used by a lot of the good players today. Top players, including Jack Nicklaus for one, and myself (chuckle) use the INTERLOCKING grip, while the TEN FINGERED grip, also called the BASEBALL grip, still has a few advocates too.

The invention of the VARDON grip is attributed to the legendary Harry Vardon. Harry was a true innovator in the game, who has been said to have also developed an Over-the-neck-muzzle grab for dislodging a ball from the jaws of a dog, a One-Stranglehold for persuading recalcitrant (stubborn, resistant to authority, unruly) golfers to re-compute the totals on their scorecard, and a Two-Handed Throat grasp for throttling a caddie. But of course I don't believe any of this.

The baseball grip has both hands apart except for the left index finger of the left hand is touching the little finger of the right hand. Most players that I have talked with, that use this grip seem to think that it provides more power. "*It is wrong for a person to think power comes primarily from strong hands and strong arms. It absolutely does not! Power in the golf shot comes from body action. The function of the hands is simply to square the face, not provide the power.*" Anon[4]

The interlocking grip is probably the most effective grip because it becomes the closest to having both hands working together as one unit. *"You get rewarded at the bottom end of the club by what you do at the top end."* Jerry Barber[4]

The grip pressure should be firm but not too tight, with your elbows and shoulders slightly relaxed. At first, grip the club gently as you address the ball. This will allow you a tension-free set up. Then firm up your grip before you begin your back swing. Remember to keep the grip pressure consistent though out the swing, do not loosen your grip at the top and re-grip just prior to the forward-swing. Releasing the grip at the top of the swing is called the Piccolo because it looks like your fingers are playing a piccolo or flute. Re-gripping at the top of the swing will cause you to over tense and swing harder than you should on the down swing, which in most cases causes the club head to dig into the ground prior to the impact with the ball. Lighter the grip pressure the easier the swing resulting in greater distance and more control.

One other very important item about the grip is the position of the thumbs. The grip should be a thumbless grip, that is, the thumbs off the center of the shaft and hence out of a controlling posture. If either thumb is placed on the center of the shaft (such as the right thumb on the top of the shaft), it indicates that the golfer is trying to control the club shaft with that thumb and rather than with the fingers. At best, the thumb has a tendency to press in a downward direction and it cannot control the shaft of the club except to push it into the ground. At worst, the right thumb may be rolled under in order to get more "power" and longer distance but will only open the club face at impact and deflect the ball to the right. In either instance, if the club head does not return to the initial position through the swing it is simply uncontrollable.

It is my opinion that the left hand and your left side is the direction control of the shaft and club head, hence the ball direction, while the right hand is for the club head rotational control through the rolling and pushing of the shaft by the first three fingers of the right hand, not the thumb. *"I have discovered that by keeping the back of my left hand toward my objective--from the time the club head entered the hitting area--until it had completed the early stages of the follow-through, I naturally increase my accuracy. The full swing is the same with all clubs. I don't feel the iron swing is basically any different than the swing you use with a wood...you should not consciously try to make any modifications."* Byron Nelson[4]

"Yes, you're probably right about the left hand, but the fact is that I take the checks with my right hand." Bobby Locke, commenting on the criticism of his left-hand grip position[4].

The size of the golf club grip is also very important to the golf swing. If the grip is too thick or oversized for the players hand size the swing of the club becomes more difficult to control due to the tendency to grip the bigger grip with more pressure. A secondary problem is that larger grips will cause the club grip to extend more into the palm of the hand and less in the fingers. Control of the club swing becomes more difficult. An undersized grip will also result in the swing problems.

With today's technology and the great equipment available to club repairmen, the size of the club's grip can be adjusted in steps of 1/64th of an inch. Therefore there is very little reason to not have club grips sized to the perfect fit for any golfer.

As a master club repairman, I can wrap clubs to within a few thousandths of an inch of the size desired by the golfer and match his whole set to the same tolerance. Any club repair shop should be able to measure for the correct grip size and wrap the clubs to achieve that sizing within a very small tolerance. I cannot stress the importance of the golf clubs grip size enough. If this problem is not corrected first, no matter how much instruction is given, swing problems will always be generated.

Another item to consider is: how easy is it to maintain a good grip the club with the type of grips that are on your clubs? Old grips get worn and become slick and hard to hang on to without a high tension grasp. Re-grip your clubs every year, even twice a year to maintain the tacky feeling of the grip. This is important so you need not increase your tension on the club due to slick or worn grips. If you don't get your clubs re-gripped very often, at least wash the grips off once in a while with a firm brush and soapy water. This will remove most dirt and oil and make the grip tackier.

When selecting new grip for your clubs, select the type (wrap or nonwrap) the suits your feel and the design and material that allows you to grip the club with comfort and minimal effort. This should be determined by you and your club repairman or if you do-it-yourself, check with your teaching professional or professional club repairman for correct sizing and grip type availability.

CHAPTER IX

Practice, Practice, Practice"

WARM-UP AND PRACTICE

"People are always wondering who's better, Hogan or Nicklaus. Well I've seen Jack Nicklaus watch Ben Hogan practice, but I've never seen Ben watch anybody practice. What's that tell you?" Tommy Bolt[1]

"They say Sam Snead is a natural golfer. But if he didn't practice, he'd be a natural bad golfer." Gary Player, on the necessity of practice[5]

Warming up, or getting loose is important to good golf. You have to stretch and exercise the muscles that you will be using during a golf swing. The goals of your golf-related exercises should be strong legs and supple upper body muscles. Stretching and slow movements promote good golf fitness.

"The purpose of practice is to tell the brain as accurately as possible, how to organize the movements of the body." John Syer & Christopher Connally.[20]

When making a swing change or just warming-up, practice by taking swings with two clubs in your hands. Added weight will help stretch your muscles and make the change back to one club easy. Sometimes you may have noted as I have, that it takes playing the first 17 holes to really get warmed up no matter what you do. When you're out of shape or just overly mature (I'm only old in body not mind) it does take longer to wake up your muscle memory. *"I figure practice puts your brains in your muscles."* Sam Snead[20] *"I think my muscle memory has developed dementia."* Bob Glanville

Practice swings (including woods, irons, wedges, and even the putter) before a game should be for establishing your rhythm, tempo and touch (getting the feel of the club as to how far a club will move the ball). Practice your short game on a 3-to-1 basis over your long game. Putting, pitching/chipping, and sand play is when strokes can be saved and feel is established.

When practicing, concentrate on just one thing in your swing or on specific golf shots that you want to make. Make sure that you have a specific goal to obtain and concentrate on that. Swing every practice shot toward a specific target. Never practice without a specific target and never practice without the knowledge of what you are trying to achieve. Aimless practice is a mistake and will transfer errors to your swing and ball direction during play.

> *"I never hit a shot, not even in practice without having a very sharp, in-focus picture of it in my head."* Jack Nicklaus[20]

When going out to practice, there is a tendency to think that the more balls I hit the greater the value of the session. Remember that you are practicing a swing that accomplishes a goal and the flight of the ball is only a visual indication that your swing is correct or not. It is important when hitting about 100 balls in the space of time, to give each swing an individual thought. Make each swing like it was a tournament winner.

When you start your warm-up, do it with short wedge shots. Gradually work up to the longer irons and hit just a few drives. Then finish off with some more wedge shots in order to keep the tempo and touch of the short game. If you find yourself in a slump, go to a driving range and just hit a pitching wedge to about 50 yards. Concentrate on tempo for half to full swings both to a complete follow-through.

SWINGING HEAVY CLUBS

If you use some type of swing weight on your club or if you own a heavy weighted practice club it is good except do not use it prior to play, only prior to practice. Do not swing the weighted club hard or you may pull a muscle or place extra stress on your back, shoulders, wrists, and arms. Swing it slowly and fully to loosen and stretch not build strength. A slow motion swing will help develop the right muscles you need but should be accomplished prior to practice not play.

In golf, you don't want muscles that are used to lift weights, you need muscles that are used to pop a whip, cast a fishing lure, or swing a baseball bat. Strong wrists, forearms, and legs are the prime necessary strong muscles needed.

<u>THE PRACTICE SWING ON THE COURSE</u>

Your practice swing should have a clear purpose whether it is a full swing or a shorter version of it. A practice swing prior to a on-the-course shot primarily is for setting your tempo and the beginning of your pre-shot routine.

A full practice swing should be a carbon copy of your hitting swing. The only difference is that one will have a ball in the club head's path. Don't let the lack of pressure due to the absence of a golf ball bother your swing or don't let the pressure of having the presents of a golf ball bother your swing.

A smaller swing, such as a half or three-quarter swing still sets your tempo. Most important in all practice swings, whether full or partial, is to complete a full follow-through.

When taking a practice swing, pick a target and swing at it. Aiming at something will help you learn to square the club head and stance. Take only one or at the most two practice swings for any more is useless and a waste of time. If taking two practice swings insure both are at the same tempo and the same size swing.

CHAPTER X

"Playing The Game Mentally"

BEATING THE GAME OF GOLF

"I don't think I've ever gotten scared on a golf course. After all, what is there to be scared of? I'm not going to die or lose my family, not even all my money. It's first a game." Ray Floyd[4]

Golf is probably the only game that a man cannot beat. How can you beat a game that has a 32 for a perfect score? That's the lowest possible score for an 18-hole course with a rating of par 72. This is considering that every Par 3 and 4 can be eagled and all of the par 5's can be double eagled. Even if every hole was birdied, the best score you can get is a 54, five shots below the 59, the recorded best round that any professional has ever shot in a PGA professional sanctioned tournament.

That "Best Score" is 13 under par 72 or 12 under par 71, or 11 under par 70 or well you get the picture. It was first accomplished by Al Gieberger in the second round of the Danny Thomas Memphis Classic in 1977. It was later matched by Chip Beck in 1991, by David Duval in 1999, by Annika Sorenstam in 2001, and by Phil Mickelson at the Grand Slam of Golf in 2005. By the way, Phil missed a 4 foot curling birdie putt on the 18th hole to end up with his 59. He could have been the only one ever to shoot a 58. Most recent 59 was by Paul Goydos playing in the John Deere Classic in July 2010.

Men can beat other men at golf, but they cannot beat the game, only get better at it as they play more. That then is the goal, not to beat the game, but only to be better than anyone else. Usually a golf match is a test of your skill against your opponent's luck.[26]

Consistency in golf will improve when a player sorts out what is important and what isn't. Remember that the game of <u>golf</u> is swinging a club not hitting a ball. Decide what has to be done; do it, and don't worry about the rest. Then, realize that it's not going to be perfect.[27]

"Golfers who try to make everything perfect before taking the shot rarely make a perfect shot." www.com

GOOD GOLF VS REAL GOLF [26]

"Golf is hard," non-golfers say. *"I don't have the patience."* Come on folks, golf is not hard. College Calculus is hard. Explaining how concrete sailboats float is hard. By comparison, golf is no sweat.

Non-golfers think golf is hard because they fail to differentiate between good golf and real golf. They are widely different things.

Good golf is the domain of people who have:

1. Abnormal, even freakish levels of patience, concentration, and persistence.
2. Time, money and/or a forgiving spouse, in varying large amounts.
3. That uncanny ability to shut off the consciousness and let the subconscious work.

Real golf is what the other 99 percent of the golfing public plays. They hack, duff, shank, shimmy, skull, sky, blade, chunk, chili-dip, worm-burn, snap-hook, duck-hook, whiff mulligan, Alice, yip, gimme, push, slice, dice, and chop their way to an altogether different and much more comfortable spiritual plane. Real golf is the game of the people. Now that's my kind of living at my age.

Hank Aaron: *"It took me seventeen years to get 3,000 hits in baseball. I did it in one afternoon on the golf course."*

Real golfers for the most part forgo formal instruction.

Ultimately, all lessons and practice suck precious time away from the beloved golf course. Besides, real golfers don't need lessons to play better, they just need better equipment.

Real golfers have fun, usually from laughing at themselves. A playing partner of a real golfer had made a career out of a beautiful, smooth, controlled tempo practice swing, a practice swing that is completely forgotten seconds later in the psychotic fury of his real hitting swing. The split second at the pinnacle of his motion when he loses control is palpable: His face mutates like film actor Lon Chaney Jr's in accelerated time lapse as in the old movie "Werewolf". The driver head vibrates briefly but violently and despite a club speed of 355 mile per hour, he toe shanks the ball into a bush five yards off the tee box. Snickers are stifled for all of three seconds, then the rest of his foursome cracks up laughing.

Real golfers are secure in their station is life. They don't cheat, although they do play winter rules for all but a three-day period in late June. Real golfers don't lie about their games, at least until they get home. Their prime concern is if the new ice chest will fit into the cart basket, they savor dawdling over Xed-out balls they find, they remember hitting a drive on the screws, not that they triple-bogeyed the last hole, and they enjoy watching the movie "Caddyshack."

For good golfers, none of this is possible. They worry about head being still, hip turn, weight shift, and a firm left side. They carry heavy luggage, complain about paying $87 for a dozen balatas, and hit 16 greens in regulation and grumble, "I couldn't make a putt."

Real golf isn't hard, only good golf is hard.

Willie Nelson speaking about his own golf course in Austin, Texas: "*Its my own damn course, and I can do anything I feel like out there,* " he explains. "*I can wear what I want. Drink what I want. Play with who I want and not play with who I don't want to play with. Par is whatever I say it is. I've got one hole that's a par 23, and yesterday I damn near birdied the sucker.*"[5]

Perhaps the first task for the aspiring golf player wishing to better his game is to become aware of the mental factors roused by the game of golf. I found them to be many and multifaceted, but essentially they seemed to fall into five categories:

The lure of the game to the ego: the seductive quality.
The precision it requires.

The competitive pressures placed on the golfer.

The unique pace of the game.

The continuing obsession with the mechanics of the swing.

Having said all that about the mental part of the game let us regress a little and look at a realistic point of view about the mentality of the game of golf.

<u>THE MENTAL GAME OF GOLF</u>[25]

The first quote of this book (page xvii) I got from an email sent to me. I don't know who sent it or who said it, but my first guess is that it might be a pearl of wisdom from the great Yogi Berra. At first, I included it because it seemed humorous, but the more I thought about it the more I deduced that there is a very important lesson to be learned from this simple statement: "*The game of Golf is 90% mental and 10% mental.*"

We travel through this world each and every day allowing our subconscious to do its thing. For example, we walk, talk, breath, and move all without even applying a conscious thought to it. We don't tell our legs how to move to walk it is something we have learned as a baby by trial and error. We get up we fall down until we take the first step. Then we do it all over again and again until it becomes second nature a learned function and stored in memory (muscle memory). Now all we do is have a conscious thought about wanting to walk, which translates to our subconscious as a goal to reach and it takes over and controls the body as to what to do to accomplish the goal of walking. On the average, about 90% of our brain is used by the subconscious to perform all the actions our bodies are taught to do which now includes how to swing a golf club. It receives input from the conscious portion of our brain through our five senses to correct and up-date the input data to help the subconscious to obtain the goal which is: swinging a club not hitting a ball.

What about the other 10%? Well that is our conscious portion of the brain that we use to react to the five senses of sight, feel, taste, hearing, and smell. It is the place where our emotions evolve (fear, love, desires, etc), where analytical processes begin, and sensory input are processed and sent to the subconscious. We use our consciousness for deductive reasoning, that thought process that normally keeps us safe and out of trouble. But, that's before we get to the golf course!

NOT A NEW CONCEPT!

Back in 1992, in his book "The Golf Secrets of the Big-Money Pros" in Part 3, "the Secrets of Psychology & Mental Preparation," Jerry Heard states quote: "I've heard it said that once you've learned how to play, the game of Golf is about 95% mental. There's really a lot of truth to that." Unquote[30]. I think he's 5% short but on the mark as to concept.

He goes on to talk about: "Keep it in Perspective" in other words, play your game, "Even Out The Highs and Lows" all shots are of the same value and require the same level of concentration, and finally "Focus In – Focus Out" this is where he stresses concentration. Quote: "Focus In. You focus on your key swing thought and nothing else gets in your mind for the next 3 or 4 seconds". Unquote.

Mr. Heard pin points actual swing time (2 to 3 seconds) while I stress part of the set up routine as part of the overall swing, hence I suggest 4 to 6 seconds from start to finish. Either way, it is the same concept: Concentrate on your swing nothing else. He then goes on to point out the importance of "Visualization" being part of the "Focus Out" aspect of his teachings. I agree with the two parts of the Focus Out mentality whereas the first part talks about the time after a shot has been made being used to concentrate on the next one as you are walking up to the ball. The second part is after selecting your club, standing behind the ball and visualizing the shot! Whoa, this is where I have to step in and say that what you visualize must mean something to the subconscious so it can relate the information to an action it is suppose to provide, swing a club.

The visualization should be a preliminary stepping through your swing components which provides a quick review for the subconscious as to what it will be expected to perform after you set up for the swing and begin to order the execution of it. It cannot process the thoughts of a ball flight to a green when it cannot see either, therefore it must revert back to muscle memory to execute a swing that will probably be centered on hitting the ball rather than making a proper swing through it. That's when you get into trouble and because your concentration is not Focused In but still Focused Out. Your concentration or conscious thoughts should be a focused control of the swing that provides the subconscious feedback so it can perform the tasks as you provide such as: Start backswing low and slow all the way to the top, drop hands down and complete the swing by breaking the wrists, accelerating through the ball position and finishing high with your belly button point toward the hole. Smile, you just did it right and that happy feeling is an adrenaline to the subconscious. Now that is something for it to remember and repeat time and time again.

If we can teach our subconscious how to get the body to walk as a baby, why can't we teach it how to swing a golf club the same way time after time as an adult? Therein lays the problem we must over come. We, as adults, can but we don't. Why? Because, of the many more factors involved in swinging a golf club than there is walking. Factors like: "how much money can I lose?"; "is this going to hurt by back?"; "is anybody watching me?"; and "I can't do this because…..". Sound familiar? And, we haven't even started on the mechanics of the swing and its problems yet!

What is the solution then? Well it is simple, do what you did as a baby. Try, and when you fall down, get up and try again. If you continue trying, you will eventually teach your subconscious how to swing a golf club the way it satisfies your game. The professional and scientific term for this activity is called "Practice". Learn to "Lessen Your Failures. Remember this book's title?

Ok, so now we have our subconscious trained, but what about the other mental aspect of golf? That conscious 10% of our brain we have to deal with, but more importantly, that we must control. Well, being an Engineer by trade, here is my solution: "$\Delta d + (! \times [\$] \& * ?) = c\#$". This is my formula for the most important question you ask yourself during a game of golf: "What club should I use?"

Let me explain the aspects of this formula for you. The symbol Δ is the Greek symbol or letter "delta" which in mathematics represents a "change" or a "changing value." The closely following letter "d" represents "distance" and used with the symbol delta, to mean a "changing distance". This is the first and hopefully only factor necessary in selecting a club for a golf shot. The term "changing distance" is that distance from the pin that the ball must travel in order to get to the hole. It is a changing value because it must take into account such things as; the wind direction and force, the location of the green as to elevation from where your ball lies and the lie of your ball whether it is in the fairway or in deep grass. Since the actual ground distance to the pin is always consistent (at the 150 yard marker, its 150 yards to the middle of the green) and therefore the distance covered by the flight of the ball must be the same. But, there are those other variables that must be considered because it may take a 5 to 8 iron to hit 150 yards under various weather conditions.

Therefore the selection of the right club to be used must take into account all the factors that will help or hinder the flight of the ball to satisfy Δd.

The term"+" simply means that in addition to Δd there are mental factors (other than those noted above involving Mother nature.) that will affect the selection of a golf club for a particular shot. These terms, enclosed in parentheses, normally should not even be considered but because of our unique ability to <u>not</u> control our conscious thought, they appear and affect our reasoning which in turn causes a lack of or decrease in our concentration ability.

These terms are:

!   The exclamation point represents "stress." We have a tendency to put more importance on a particular golf shot than on others. The importance can be monetary or egotistical. Stress will normally shorten a back swing due to tensing of the muscles in the neck and back and gritting of teeth, all of which results in a varying distance the ball travels.

x   The small x represents a multiplication factor. Stress will increase when multiplied by the amount of money involved or importance of the game or tournament being played.

[ ]   The brackets are used to isolate the money value as being the only value that will multiply the stress factor more than any other.

$ The small dollar sign represents the monetary importance of the shot. How much money will be won or lost. The dollar sign will get bigger and bigger as the monetary value increases and multiplies stress. When in a "press" situation, incorrect clubs can be selected to "play it safe." This value could relate closely to the "need to win factor" or notoriety.

&   The ampersand just means "plus" which means that the following terms also add to the stress but not effect it as much as the monetary value.

*   The asterisk represents "stardom" or the "I must win" or worse yet the "I'm as good as the pro's are" syndrome. An emotional importance, that closely ties in with the ego. Ego will normally get a player to attempt more difficult shots with inadequate clubs because "if Tiger Woods can do it, so can I!"

?   The question mark represents the "questionable" aspects and doubts of the player. "How do I feel?" Confident? Not too sure?

Back hurt? Can't see to good? Can I really make this shot from here? All the questions that you allow to arise that causes doubt in your ability to make the correct swing.

= The equal sign points to the solution of the equation, "selected club number C#."

If we can consciously minimize all the factors to the right side of the plus sign and rely on our subconscious, club selection and most golf shots would be very satisfying. But, we are human, after all, so the formula sometimes gets out of whack and all scrambled up due to over analysis or stress and becomes:

$$(\# +] * ?) \times \$] = \text{"d"}$$

The true meaning of the formula is now lost. But, the English translation of what has been scrambled is now found in the mind of most golfers and often spoken loudly in French immediately after executing a bad shot due to wrong club selection and throwing said wrong selected club in a nearby lake. Now term "d" simply means "disaster" or a new term for the wayward club: "Dunker".

It is not hard to teach your subconscious, hence your body to swing a golf club. You learned to walk didn't you? It is harder to teach yourself, self control, than it is to learn to swing a club. But, it can be done. It just takes persistence during swing practice, dedication and help from a professional.

It is also possible to teach your mind to focus. It too just takes persistence in practicing mental discipline, dedication to self control and as a last ditch effort, to go to get a little help from a psychiatric specialist (review definition of golf analyst on page 3).

SEDUCTIVE QUALITY

"Golf is not a funeral, although both can be very sad affairs." Bernard Darwin[5]

There is a seductive quality to golf. In moments of frustration many players vow to quit, but only a few are able to. For some reason, the two or three "triumphs" experienced during a round are remembered long after the exasperating failures and dull mediocrities are forgotten. In my case, it is the challenge that golf provides. Every drive, fairway shot, approach shot, and putt is a different experience, even on a hole that you have played over and over again.

Some of the attraction of the game lay in the fact that golf is one of the few sports that a novice can, on occasion, perform like a champion. The sight of the ball soaring high and true is exhilarating. It fills you with a sense of mastery and power. But, it is also true that golf is very frustrating and that too is one of the compelling attractions to the game. *"Golf's a hard game to figure. One day you'll go out and slice it and shank it, hit into all the traps and miss every green. The next day you go out and for no reason at all you really stink."* www.com

The frustration is that you cannot repeat the experience of a great shot at will. Golf seems to rise up hopes, only to dash them and to puff-up an ego, only to squash it again, over and over. As I see it, there are five stages of a golfer's game: Sudden Collapse, Radical Change, Complete Frustration, Slow Improvement, Brief Mastery, and Sudden Collapse. *"Golf is the hardest game in the world. There's no way you can ever get it. Just when you think you do, the game jumps up and puts you into your place."* Ben Crenshaw[5]

PRECISION

The most agonizing aspect of the game is clearly its inconsistency. Therefore, the precision required to play good golf demands much greater mental discipline that is necessary in many other sports. The precision required in golf doesn't always allow for release of pent-up anger and frustration.

Golf produces frustration, but requires that you learn to deal with it in some way other than in your next shot. This presents the mental challenge. Expert psychologists say that external denial is good for the golfer. A golfer should accept the internal success of a great shot but deny that a missed shot is his fault. All great golfers have done it and most of the players on the professional tours still do it.

The failure to make a shot can be blamed on an external cause rather than accepting it internally as a failure or as a lack of ability or concentration. It is healthy to find that external source and vent the frustration immediately rather than carry it to the next shot. It could be a noise from the crowd, or an airplane, or the "blimp". It could be the glint of the putter from the sun just before the take-away or someone's shadow or a movement of another player, or even the click of a camera. External denial helps to clear the frustration and vent anger before it builds up to an uncontrollable level.

"Everyone has his own choking level, a level at which he fails to play his normal golf. As you get more experience, your choking level rises." Johnny Miller[4]

CONCENTRATION[17]

"Thinking must be the hardest thing we do in golf, because we do so little of it." Harvey Penick[1]

I normally would never disagree with the likes of Harvey Penick but this quote would be truer if the word "thinking" were replaced by the word "concentration". We think way too much and don't do near enough concentrating. But, that's normal because the time allowed for us to think verses the time allowed to concentrate is at a ratio of about 25 to 1. 250 minutes in a round of golf to think, analyze, and agonize versus the total of 10 minutes we need to concentrate during all of our swings.

The ability to concentrate is vital to every golfer's performance. By understanding how your personality and tendencies affect your ability to concentrate and then adopting the appropriate mental techniques, you can enhance your ability to concentrate when you need it the most.

Concentration is nothing more than focusing your complete and undivided attention upon the objects of your choice. Focusing awareness always involves choice. The most common reason for loss of focus among golfers is that they become either too relaxed or too tense during play, hence choose to think rather than concentrate.

If too relaxed your thoughts tend to wander and you simply go through the motions of playing with little focus and lots of hope that your body will do all the work necessary to play good golf. If you are too tense, your focus tends to jump around, making you aware of too many things, e.g., noise, movement, trouble spots, golf swing mechanics and so on. Consider using thought-stopping and relaxation techniques during your round (you can find many self-help books and tapes on these subjects in your local bookstore or library). Such techniques can help you to find the source of your tension and reduce it appropriately.

It is impossible to learn concentration without practicing it, and it is not until you start practicing it that you become aware what it is, what its benefits are, and perhaps how concentrated you have been. Concentration usually occurs when you allow – not force – yourself to become interested in something.

Analysis and mechanics run close second behind tension as the most common deterrent to concentration. A players who is obsessed with finding, correcting, and improving his swing or stroke, during their every round, are essentially playing "Golf Swing" rather than playing golf. These players analyze their way around the course with little awareness of target, visualization, tempo, feel, or touch.

While analysis is the first step of any good mental routine used to narrow your focus, the analysis must end before you set up to the ball, and you should work on your mechanics before and after but never during competition.

Once you have dealt with some of your distracting tendencies, you will want to strengthen your concentration skills. The most important techniques for attaining full concentration involve the development of a strong pre-shot routine that must be used before every shot or putt.

If you incorporate the following three mental steps into your physical routine, and use them consistently, you'll find that your ability to concentrate will improve dramatically.

(1) Calculation: Narrow your focus and turn your thoughts to the next swing. This involves quickly, sorting through analytical details such as wind factor (and other facets of Mother Nature), lie, yardage target line, type of shot required, and club selection (see my formula on page 94). Then commit fully to your club selection, the target line, and the type of swing you will require to accomplish your objective.
(2) Feel: Practice the swing you are going to use. Swing as if you are going to actually impact a ball with it.
(3) Trust: Know that your swing can and will do the job, then let it.

Visualization: Narrow your focus more by standing behind your ball and clearly seeing your target. Then visualize as clearly as possible the swing you want to make to cause the flight of your ball for the result desired. Then approach your address with this conviction and self control. This is where you begin you 4 – 6 seconds of concentration on accomplishing your swing, not hitting the ball, utilizing your mental discipline and subconscious abilities. Golf is 90% mental (Subconscious: muscle memory) and 10% mental (Conscious: sensory) discipline.

<u>COMPETITION</u>

The competition of golf lies in the following areas: the first is playing against others, and the second, which is incorporated into the first, is playing against yourself and the course. In either case, every shot counts. Golf does not forgive mistakes, thus the pressure is always constant. *"Golf is the only sport where the most feared opponent is you"*. www.com

The golf score is a pretty true indication of skill. Even so, this pressure attracts golfers to the game. As a rule, most golfers prefer the tougher course to play, rather than easy ones. They will play from the back tees where the pros play so they can compare their skill with the "Big Boys" without playing against them. They like to add to the pressure of playing by betting money on the outcome (sometimes it's on every shot or every hole and /or overall total strokes),"just to make it more interesting."

Learning to play under this pressure is the mental challenge and when it comes to sinking a five foot putt on the last hole to win by one shot, it becomes a lot more mental than physical.

"Most golfers prepare for disaster. A good player prepares for success."
Bob Toski[4]

It is probably every golfer's dream to play in and win the "Big" one. We dream about winning the U.S. Open or maybe the Masters, but no matter what the level of competition, the idea is to play the best we can and win. Here are some tips about playing competitive or pressure golf:

Before you begin a competitive round, set a goal of playing the entire round with one swing and one tempo without reacting to any single putt or shot. Commit to your plan and visualize playing each hole individually. Change your plan only if circumstances that are out of your control, makes it necessary.

Think positive and keep a good mental attitude. Remember that you are playing where you are at because you were good enough to get there.

"...the tournament professional survives by confidence and so must never allow thoughts of his own fallibility to penetrate his consciousness

from any source...he has to believe in his prowess because that faith in himself is his greatest asset." Arnold Palmer[4]

Other players have their own doubts about themselves and you so don't help them by doubting yourself or allowing them to convince you that they are better than you.

"The person I fear the most in the last two rounds is myself". Tom Watson[4]

Play within your own game. Don't try to match your opponent's long drives, iron shots, or putting. Play within your abilities, swing and tempo. A quote by Bobby Jones, after watching Jack Nicklaus win the 1965 Masters: *"He plays a game with which I'm not familiar."*[5]

"Good players aren't worried about what anybody else thinks of them. They don't want to APPEAR to be mentally tough, they want to BE mentally tough. And they do that by playing their own game, shot by shot, at their own pace and tempo." Dr Bob Rotella[4]

Stay away from vanity. Vanity often urges you to try a shot which is outside your ability but within the ability of a class player such as Jack Nicklaus or Arnie Palmer. Remember that "Asking more than your best will produce the worst." If you chance a "risky" shot, more times than not you will fail and it may result in a loss of confidence of your real abilities. Even if you make the shot, you may build false confidences which may cost you dearly in future rounds.

A very critical thing to remember is that the most important shot in golf is ....??

"THE NEXT ONE" There is only one important golf shot in golf and that is the one that you are about to hit, there is nothing else. The past shots are history. The ones after the next one are a mystery. So, play the shot that is present and accept it as a gift to enjoy

If you hit a poor shot, don't try to hit a miracle shot to make up for it. *"When you miss a shot, never think of what you did wrong. Come up to the next shot thinking of what you must do right...The average expert player—if he is lucky—hits six, eight or ten good shots a round. The rest are good misses."* Tommy Armour[4]

" *If your afraid that a full shot might reach the green while the foursome ahead of you is still putting out, you have two options: you can immediately shank a lay-up, or you can wait until the green is clear and top the ball halfway there.*" www.com

PACE OF THE GAME

Refer to Chapter III. The best thing here to remember is that golf is only played during a single 4 - 6 second period. That is about the average time it takes to set up and perform a golf swing. Its the time between shots that we must control and prepare mentally for. All that other time in the round of golf is where you keep pace with the group ahead. That is where we convince ourselves that we are good enough or not, to play the game.

COURSE MANAGEMENT DURING PLAY

"My body is here, but my mind has already teed off." www.com

"Once you have learned how to strike a ball, course management and psychology become the dominate factors in successfully playing the game. If you can't manage yourself and the course, you can't play." Harvey Penick[20]

Course management concerns club selection, time awareness, and type of shot to be made. Choosing what shot to make either cuts your score or quickly adds to it. There is more to golf than just hitting a golf ball a long way. There is judgment of distance and how hard the ball could be hit for a given distance and under different circumstances.

This capability comes from experience, usually from practice and lessons, but mostly from lots of play. It is important to manage the course and not let it manage you.

Here are some tips to help you play a course better with practice. For without practice, nothing becomes better.

1. When you play a course and expect to play it again, keep a book on it. Write down distances and clubs used and specific features of each hole.
2. If your on a new course, always go to the practice green first and practice chipping and putting.

3. When playing on a course the first time or if it is a practice round, try hitting your approach shots with one more club than what you would normally hit.
4. Lay up on blind shots unless you know your landing area.
5. If the course has deep rough, always use a lofted wood to hit out of it.
6. Your target for all approach shots should be center of green no matter where the pin is cut.
7. If the course has narrow fairways, use a more controllable club if you are not accurate with the driver.
8. Trust and rely on your swing to get you through the day.

"Learn one basic shot and stick with it, one you can hit under pressure. If you have a good basic shot you'll rarely have to hit a fancy one."
Anon

On the lighter side, have you noticed that no matter how early your tee time is, there will always be a foursome in the middle of the first fairway? Also that if you par the first three holes you will have a 20 minute wait on the fourth tee box?

Why is the public course's golf shop supply and demand always the same where as:

1. They have extra spikes, but they don't fit your shoes?
2. They have the kind of golf glove you like, but not in your size?
3. All the hats are yellow, never fit, and melt in the rain.
4. The only cheap golf balls are used ones with your mark on them.
5. The only available tee times are 5 am or 4 pm?
6. The have an over stock of cheap umbrellas until it rains?
7. Rain checks are only good on other rainy days?

"Golf is a game which the slowest people in the world are those in front of you, and the fastest are those behind" www.com

THE MECHANICS OF THE SWING

There will be more about the golf swing in Chapter XI, but for now let me say that most of the problems in a golf swing is our inability to concentrate on the things necessary to accomplish a physical movement that should be natural and easy. You may ask, "How can anyone remember all there is to know about the golf swing and recall them all in a short 4 - 6 second period?" Well no one can and no one is expected to.

The swing should include only two things, the take-away or back-swing and the forward-swing to a full follow-through. Notice I didn't mention anything about hitting a ball, that is accomplished somewhere in the forward-swing. So, the mechanics of a swing boils down to taking the club back into a position to accomplish a forward-swing and then swing the club to a full follow-through. Most of these actions are physical and require very little conscious mental ability. You don't have to remember everything, just a couple a things (one or two in the back-swing and one or two in the forward-swing) to accomplish the swing and hence the movement of the ball.

Everyone has the natural ability to swing a club. No two golfer's swings are perfectly alike. They are as unique as the individual who uses them. All golf swings do not have to be perfect (no such thing anyway) or pretty, just functional. Just watch some of the pros and you will see some really unique, even ugly swings, but they work.

"If a great golf swing puts you high on the money list, there'd be some of us who would go broke." Ray Floyd[4]

CHAPTER XI

"The Perfect Golf Swing Is A Myth."

THE MECHANICS

"I found out that all the important lessons of life are contained in the three rules for achieving a perfect golf swing:

1. *Keep your head down.*
2. *Follow through.*
3. *Be born with money."* www.com

Literally hundreds of books and magazine articles have been written in the last 60 years or so about the mechanics of the golf swing, and more on the same continues to roll off the presses almost every day. Volumes upon volumes, videos by the hundreds and even audio tapes provide all the information necessary to achieve the perfect swing, which leads one to conclude that the only people who aren't proficient at the game are rank beginners or those who can't see, read or hear.[28] Unfortunately, people are different therefore a useable single perfect swing is a myth. One must also conclude that there is no one perfect swing for everybody, but everybody has a swing that could be made perfect for them. I don't teach people my swing, although some have tried to copy or imitate it to no avail. Their own swing seemed to work very well, once shown that they have a good swing of their own, but needed to be taught how to use it to their advantage and within their own capabilities.

"Those commonalities of the good players are the basic fundamentals of golf techniques. They haven't changed much in an awful long time, and they aren't a whole lot of them. But they have to be understood and mastered if you are to play the game consistently at or close to the maximum of your potential." Jack Grout[20]

It is not difficult to see how superstition thrives, for so many players are in constant search of "The Secret" and endless magic formulas are propagated by true believers and golfers are ready to try anything to relieve frustration. The golfer finds his hope raising as he hits a few good shots after trying a given tip. It works!! He thinks, but then "The Secret" is dropped after a few poor shots. Hope wanes and frustration begins to set in again. He is now ready and eager for the next tip.

"You have to make corrections in your game a little bit at a time. It's like taking your medicine. A few aspirin will probably cure what ails you, but the whole bottle might just kill you." Harvey Penick[20]

"His swing reminds me a lot of a machine I once saw at a county fair making saltwater taffy. It goes in four directions and none of them seem right." Buck Adams on Miller Barber's swing.[5]

The happiest and best golfers realize that there is no single gimmick that works, and that good golf is attained only by patience and humility and by continually practicing both the outer game of mechanics and the mental game skills of Concentration, Confidence, and Willpower (self control).

THE MYTHICAL PERFECT SWING[28]

The point is that it doesn't matter if you look like a beast before or after the hit, as long as you look like a beauty at the moment of impact." Seve Balleteros[4]

"Reverse every natural instinct and do the opposite of what you are inclined to do, and you will probably come very close to having a perfect golf swing." Ben Hogan[29]

The first steps of your perfect swing are to establish the correct grip and the proper stance or address which includes correct body alignment to ball and target line. Once the address is established, a very slight press forward is a good beginning of the swing and helps to begin a slow smooth take away. Waggle if necessary to relieve tension and stress. Begin focused concentration on swing.

The take away (back swing) ends when your back is somewhat toward the hole and the club shaft is somewhat parallel to the ground. At this point, the club shaft could be aligned with the target line (looking from the side away from the target) and the club head (toe of the club face) is pointing straight down toward the ground. Your wrists are cocked and your grip is firm. Your head is solid over the ball (could be slightly behind the ball) with your left arm fully extended. Left heel off the ground, left knee slightly toward right one and hips rotated about 45 degrees from address position.

A forward swing begins with the shoulders moving which causes the hands to drop on line about six to eight inches. The left foot's heel is replanted and then the knees, hips, and arms follow the shoulders. The hands and wrists move (wrists are uncocking) around to position the club back to original position at address (left hand controlling direction and right hand controlling club head position), then forward to the target through the ball impact area, finishing on the same plane created by the back swing. The result is a straight trajectory toward the target.

"Follow-through is an important element in skill involving powerful propulsion of an object." Tom Ecker[4]

The follow-through begins after ball impact and just past the point where your club head has reached top speed and starts slowing down. The hips are rotating out of the way, allowing the hands, arms and shoulders to fully rotate to a position where your front side (belly button) is facing the target.

"The only purpose of the golf swing is to move the club through the ball square to the target at maximum speed. How this is done is of no significance at all, so long as the method enables it to be done repetitively." John Jacobs[4]

All of these mechanics only describe how to get the club to the top of the back swing and then back down through the ball position to a follow-through. That is the perfect swing: get the club into a starting position then swing it around to a full follow-through. The simple fact is that golf is making a swing, not hitting a ball. The perfect swing is one that moves the ball to where you want it to go by just swinging the club and not by trying to hit the ball.

"The good player swings though the ball while the awkward player hits at it." Ken Venturi[4]

Here are a few quick notes for your swing:

a. Simply your golf. Everything is a result of just swinging the golf club.

b. You should never be aware of using your wrists in any golf shot. They should respond automatically to the action initiated by the hands and fingers.

c. A player who has a "mechanical" put-together swing only hits one good shot in ten and can never play well under pressure. Be flexible and use all your capabilities.

d. Brute force cannot be controlled, but you can control your swing with concentration.

"If you want to hit a 7-iron as far as Tiger Woods does, simply try to lay up short of a water hazard." www.com

e. Without good control through the hands working together it is impossible to swing a club properly. The left hand guides, the right hand strikes. That is, the right hand makes the club head catch up with the hands at the impact point and helps to accelerate the club through to a high finishing follow-through while following the left's control.

f. Exercise your hands. The body is the power unit and the hands and arms are the antennas which transmit that power. If the hands are weak, they act like a resistance to the power and transmit weak signals to the club. Many problems experienced by golfers can be corrected by simple hand and grip adjustments.

g. The practice range is the place to experiment. When playing on the course, trust your swing and have the mind only on the swinging of the club head. Any part of the body you may be thinking about is where the power will be transmitted to.

h. The foundation of a good consistent swing is keep you head still.

"If everybody could learn to hold his head still there wouldn't be any golfers around still trying to break 100." Arnold Palmer [4]

i. Be persistent. *"Nothing in the world can take the place of persistence. Talent will not; nothing is more common than unsuccessful men with talent. Genius will not; unrewarded genius is almost a proverb. Education will not; the world is full of educated derelicts. Persistence and determination alone are omnipotent. The slogan "press on" has solved and always will solve the problems of the human race."* Calvin Coolidge, 30th U.S. President[29]

"There are no secrets to success: Don't waste time looking for them. Success is the result of perfection, hard work, learning from failure, loyalty to those with whom you work, and persistence." General Colin Powell, U.S. Army (retired)[29].

CHAPTER XII

"Which Way Did the Ball Go?"

PROBLEMS

If you play poorly one day, forget it, it happens. If you play poorly two days in a row, review the basics and try again. If you play poorly the third day, go see a qualified teaching golf professional and have him look at your swing, it just may be one small thing that need be pointed out and corrected.[20]

"I'd give up golf if I didn't have so many sweaters." Bob Hope[16]

What is the problem? Problem analysis begins with knowing your swing and the basic function of the hands and grip. Having a consistent swing goes a long way in helping to eliminate problems or correcting errors. Since I stress that golf is no more than swinging a golf club, all problems stem from not swinging as you should but instead, trying to hit a ball. You do not have to have the perfect text book swing (no such thing anyway), but you do have to practice and know your swing and its capabilities. To do this will take lots of patience, practice, and someone to help point out some of the basic mechanics that your swing should follow and the development of proper concentration techniques to be repetitive.

"I am not saying my golf game went bad, but if I grew tomatoes they'd come up sliced." Lee Trevino[16]

Problems or swing mistakes, in most cases, are made before the golf club is even swung. These mistakes could include a bad grip, a misalignment in stance (either toward the target line or address to the ball), or most probable; a lack of concentration. If the problem is in the swing, tiny changes can make a big difference. The natural inclination is to overdo the tiny changes that have brought success in the past. *"Hint: any change on the course works for a maximum of three holes and a minimum of not at all." www.com*

Tempo of the swing is a major concern, so look here first for problems, sometimes you just need to slow down. Second is head position or unwanted movement of the head and shoulders (concentration and tempo helps correct this). Next would be the follow-through. Is it complete, hands high, and weight on the left side? Believe me, all problems fall into one of these six categories (grip, stance, address, tempo, head position, follow-through). The first three can be quickly eliminated with a review of your pre-shot routine. This leaves us with only three concerns to worry about.

TEMPO, HEAD POSITION, AND FOLLOW-THROUGH

"There is no one right speed for everyone…if I tried to play at his (Tom Watson's) breakneck speed…I'd self-destruct before I finish the front nine." Nancy Lopez[4]

The definition of TEMPO is: A characteristic rate or rhythm of activity; the pace set by a performer. The word TEMPO comes from the word "Temporal", which has two meanings, the first is: pertaining to, concerning with, or limited by time. The second is: comes from the temporal bones in the neck located at the base of the skull and is in very close proximity of the controlling muscles of the head.

From this definition we can deduce that the TEMPO of a golf swing is the rate or speed of the swing and the control of the position of the head. TEMPO has nothing to do with the mechanics of the swing but does affect the mechanics as it changes. For that reason alone is why this should be the first and most important item to look at when things start to go awry during play, especially as the level of competition changes, the speed of play changes, or when concentration becomes difficult due to outside influences such as noises from cars, airplanes, blimps, crowds, or other golfers.

"Golferswhotalkfastswingfast." Bob Toski[16]

Tempo for a golf swing is as individual as the swing itself.

A golfer should set a tempo according to his abilities and strengths, but once established, it should stay consistent. Tempo, as related to the time and speed of the swing, should follow the example of a drag racer where its speed is accelerating at an accelerated rate. (MPH) 10 .... 20 .... 30 ....40 ......50 .....60 ....70 .. 80 ..90 .100 .110. In this way, the club head is accelerating through the ball position and concludes with a full body turn and complete follow-through. De-acceleration of the club head should begin after ball impact not before.

"When through with practice, you have grooved a good position at the top; practically all you'll have to do to perfect your swing is to get your timing right." Anon[4]

Normally the result of golfers trying to hit a ball rather than make a swing is trying to accelerate the club head <u>to</u> the ball rather than <u>through</u> the ball position which can result in "fat" shots. If acceleration from the top is down and at a de-accelerating rate, good contact and distance is lost. Remember the drag racer? You want to accelerate to the finish line not maximize speed at the starting line. For example: (MPH) 10.20.30..40... 50...60....70.....80 ......90 ....100...........110 where all speed is during the first part of the swing and none through the ball position and follow though.

Head position controls the position of the bottom of your swing, hence the club head position in reference to the ball position. Your address to the ball set the head position and the position of the club. The swing, if made without head movement, will return the club head back to its original position which will strike the ball during the movement toward the follow-through.

The head acts as a base much like an anchored end of a pendulum. The club head is the swinging end of the pendulum arm, therefore:

> If the head moves, the bottom of the swing moves.
> Head goes up, club hits top of ball.
> Head goes down, club hits ground before ball.
> Head goes toward target, club strikes ball before being square to target and moves the ball outside the target line.

Head moves away from target, club strikes ball with club head over square position and moves ball inside the target line or tops the ball.

I hope that you can see that the flight of the ball is a visual representation of the golf swing. It can be used to detect or identify a swing problem.

"There are two thing you can do with your head down – Play golf and Pray." Lee Trevino

Follow through can be fully accomplished if the golf club is swung accelerating at an accelerated rate through the ball position. This alone requires concentration on your swing and tempo which will incorporate good head position. Swing problems are eliminated for the most part by just swinging the club and quit trying to hit the ball.

CHAPTER XIII

"Putt….Putt"

PUTTING

"Putting is like wisdom, partly a natural gift and partly the accumulation of experience." Arnold Palmer[4]

Putting styles and grips vary from individual to individual. The grip you use is important, considering that you can use the grip for putting, chipping, and pitching. Whatever grip you use, both hands should be acting as one unit. The putting stroke is a short version of the normal golf swing. For right hander's the left hand is for direction control and the right hand is to control club head position, both are used to control acceleration of the putter head through the ball position. Tempo and head position are very important in keeping the stroke smooth, unrushed and consistent.

"If there's one thing certain about putting, it is that it's an individual business. The great putters have used every conceivable type of grip, stance, and stroke." Ben Crenshaw[4]

Putting can be accomplished by used the wrists, arms, or shoulders, or a combination of each. The grip can be cross-handed or any variation of the normal vardon grip. The cross-handed grip allows the left wrist to be held more firmly through the stroke with all control (direction and club head) focused on the left hand. Another way to help eliminate a wristy putting stroke is to build up the putter's grip so that it is bigger than normal. The thicker grip on the putter will tend to restrict wrist movement and concentrate more arm and shoulders action.

"The prime requisite for putting? An abounding confidence in one's ability." Walter Travis[4]

Important tips on putting: (Remember that putting is 47% of the game of golf so commit to memory all of the following and recite each one prior to every putt!) Just kidding, but these tips will help you putt better.

1. Establish a putting routine. This helps to build confidence.
2. Concentrate on the stroke and NEVER hurry a putt.

"All I can do is start it. The Lord handles it from there." Jimmy Demaret[4]

3. Decide what you want to do then stick with it to build confidence and think POSITIVE even though.....*"The ball doesn't care how positive you are thinking when you hit it with the putter moving and aimed in the wrong direction."* Dave Pelz[4]
4. Don't worry about anything but your target line and the stroke, never think about the importance of the putt.

"Don't try too hard to hole every putt. A "must make" attitude puts too much pressure on your stroke...Just do your best to get the correct line and speed and roll the ball at the hole on that line." Ben Crenshaw[4]

5. Keep the putter low to the ground. With short putts concentrate on the line and on long putts concentrate on the distance.

"Every putt can go in, but I don't expect every putt to go in." Joan Blalock[4]

6. Play the ball somewhere between the left heel and the center of your stance. Keep your eyes directly over the ball. Playing the ball too far forward leads to inconsistency.

Sam Snead: *"These green are so fast I have to hold my putter over the ball and hit it with the shadow."*

7. Never let your right hand pass your left hand while putting. Lead with the left wrist and make sure to keep it firm. Pull the back of the left hand through the ball position and toward the target line, this will help to keep the right hand behind the left and keep it from rotating the putter face open or closed.
8. To prevent *jabbing* a putt, place more of your weight on your back foot while narrowing your stance. This will help to keep your head still and to make a smooth stroke.

"Mechanics are about 10 percent of putting...feel is 90 percent, but good mechanics lead to good feel." Tom Watson[4]

9. If your head is moving during the putting stroke, point your toes slightly outward and put more weight on the inside of your feet.
10. If your putting stroke is erratic, add weight to your putter head and concentrate on shoulder rotation and less wrist break.
11. If you are tensing up over your putts, especially the short ones take a deep breath and exhale slowly. At the end of the exhale, start your back swing slowly.

"Relax? How can anybody relax and play golf? You have to grip the club, don't you?" Ben Hogan

12. Concerning long putts:
    a. To prevent distance problems, firm up your wrists and putt using your shoulders and arms.
    b. Stand more upright. This will give you a better sense of distance and line, and will allow you a freer stroke.
    c. The only difference between a long putt and a short putt is the length of the back swing and the follow-through.

"It takes steadier nerves for that good, long stroke. A nervous individual can't putt that way." Harvey Penick[4]

A note on the size of the hole: First, consider the dimension of the golf hole and the golf ball; (A) the diameter of the hole is 4.25 inches and the diameter of the ball is 1.68 inches. Actually, only half the ball on either side of the cup is enough to tip the center of gravity and cause the ball to fall into the hole. Now, (B) you have enlarged the diameter of the hole to about 5.93 inches or by half the ball diameter on both sides.[15]

This holds true if you putt the ball to stop at the hole. The faster the ball approaches the hole, the less chance it has to fall in from the sides. If the ball is going too fast and yet over three-fourths of the ball is inside the perimeter of the hole, the ball can still "lip out" or "rim out." In this case, due to the speed of the ball, the effective diameter of the hole has been reduced to less than 1.63 inches [4.25 - 2(3/4 X 1.68)].

The faster the ball approaches the hole, the smaller the hole gets. For example, have you ever hit a putt a little harder than you wanted to and the ball went straight to the back of the cup, bounced up but stayed out on the back side? You have effectively made the size of the hole zero inches in diameter due to ball speed.

Lee Travino has observed that if a player is putting badly, then one of four things is wrong:

1. A bad stroke.
2. A bad system of planning and reading putts
3. A bad attitude.
4. A bad putter (club).[4]

Tommy Bolt: *"Putting allows the touchy golfer two to four opportunities to blow a gasket in the short space of two to forty feet."*

Jerry Heard: *"Don't make it happen – Let it happen*[30]*" Don't try to force it in there, keep your concentration on your swing from start to finish.*

CHAPTER XIV

"How Do I Get Out of Here?"

CHIPPING AND PITCHING

"Today you can drive up to the average country club practice area and see about three dinosaurs for every golfer who's out there working on pitch-and-run shots." Lee Travino[4]

What is the difference between a chip shot and a pitch? First of all, both terms are used to describe an approach shot to a green. The type of shot usually dictates what it is called, but even that doesn't keep golfers, announcers, and caddies from mixing and matching the terms.

A chip shot usually involves a very lofted club so that the ball approaches the green at a very high angle which results in very little roll after landing and even some back spin.. The L wedge, 60^0 edge or sand iron is used most often. A variation of a chip shot is the "flip shot" or "cut shot" where the ball is in deep grass but sitting up so that a lofted club could be swing under the ball causing the ball to fly out at a very steep angle.

A pitch shot involves a low trajectory which results in the ball rolling after landing on the green. A pitch shot can be accomplished using any club in the bag including the woods and Hybrids.

The first and foremost fundamental to learn about chipping or pitching is to keep your hands ahead of or at the very least, even with the club head at the impact area and into the follow-through. This will insure that you are swinging down into the ball and the club head is accelerating through the impact area giving the ball the desired back spin for drawing the ball back or causing the ball to "check-up".

The second fundamental is TEMPO which will help keep your head perfectly still. Beyond that, everything else depends on the position of the ball and the swing that will be required to get the ball onto the green and close to the hole.

"Basically I chip the way I putt...The most important factor in making the chipping stroke, I believe, is keeping both wrists fixed." Lanny Watkins[4]

Always chip a ball if under any or all of the following circumstances: you have a bad lie, the green is hard, you have a down hill lie, hitting to an down-hill sloping green, the wind is going to affect the flight of the ball, you are under stress, or when you have the feeling that chipping is better.

Always pitch a ball if under any or all of the following circumstances: you have a good lie, you are close to the putting surface, you have an up-hill lie, you are hitting to a up-hill sloping green, the green is very soft, a low shot is required due to an obstacle, or when you have the feeling that pitching is better.

GREENSIDE SAND TRAP SHOTS

"The difference between a sand bunker and water is the difference between a car crash and an airplane crash. You have a chance of recovering from a car crash." Bobby Jones[4]

Practice your green side bunker game to become more aggressive with it. If you practice and learn a few fundamentals, playing out of a bunker is not difficult, even for a average player.

Things to ponder while stepping into a green side bunker for your next shot. Is the sand wet, dry, course, fine or powdery? Is your ball buried in the sand, on top of the sand, on a down hill or up hill slope? Does the ball have to fly a long way to the hole or is it cut close to the bunker?

After taking your stance and making your decision as to the type of swing you are to make, think only of the club head accelerating toward the target line through the sand. This will get the ball out most of the time and toward the hole. Always complete the swing to a good follow through.

Too many players stop their club at the ball impact area which normally results in the ball only moving positions in the same sand trap or sailing across the green into the opposite bunker or water hazard.

Three things to accomplish when hitting from a green side sand bunker:

1. Get the ball out of the bunker. (most important)
2. Get the ball onto the putting surface.
3. Get the ball close to or into the hole.

FAIRWAY BUNKER SHOTS

If you are in a sand bunker next to the fairway use one less lofted club than you would normally use for the distance to the pin. Swing easy and within your tempo. Play the ball back in your stance and use a stiff-wristed stroke. Keep most of your weight on the back side. (The side away from the hole)

"Do not flip the wrists, the ball should come out slowly."
Gene Sarazen[4]

You must hit the ball before hitting the sand. Swing shallow, taking very little sand, you ball will fly farther with more back spin.

SPECIAL SHOTS

Special shots are those shots that are not normally used in a round of golf, but now and then we find ourselves in a situation that requires a little more thought and a little more skill to pull off a shot we would not normally practice.

"I do not advocate unorthodox golf but I make provisions for it."
Homer Kelly[4]

Here are a few that come to mind:

1. Hitting a driver off the fairway. You want more distance and lower trajectory this is the shot for you. Key to pulling this off is to swing smooth and easy. Don't try to kill the ball or swing hard to get extra distance.

2. Ball on hard ground. Play the ball back and swing shallow. You don't want a divot.

3. Ball in a divot. Play the ball back in your stance and take one more club with a lower loft. Swing normal expecting to enlarge the divot that your ball is in.

4. Ball under a tree. Hit a low punch shot. Use a 1 or 3 wood or 1, 2 or 3iron. Grip down on the club and take a short back swing, but swing to a complete follow-through as allowed by the obstacle.

5. Ball on a side hill higher than your feet. Keep your weight on your toes. Don't fall off the hill during the swing. Keeping your head very still is key. Aim to right of target line.

6. Ball on a side hill lie lower than your feet. Keep your weight on your heels. Swing smooth don't "go down after the ball." Use one more club than usual. Aim to the left of target line.

7. Ball on up-hill lie. Keep weight on up-hill foot. Aim slightly to the right of target line and swing with the contour of the ground with a less lofted club.

8. Ball on down-hill lie. Keep you weight on down-hill foot. Play ball in back of stance slightly. Swing with the contour of the ground with a more lofted club.

9. Never try shots that come off once in a life time. The only exception to this rule is when the state of the game is "Now or Never."

CHAPTER XV

"Playing Golf With Mother Nature"

"I love rotten weather. The founders of the game accepted nature for what it gave, or what it took away. Wind and rain are great challenges. They separate real golfers." Ton Watson[4]

PLAYING IN THE WIND

Playing golf in the wind is normal and usual. The wind will affect all golf shots including putting so it is important to keep your tempo, slow down and keep it smooth. The greatest effect the wind has on the ball will be during the highest point of trajectory. Look up at the top of the surrounding trees. It is at this level that the wind will have the greatest impact on the ball's flight. Don't fight the wind, you will lose the battle. Instead, learn to use it and benefit from its force on your ball and the frustration it will cause your opponent.

On a windy day:

1. When hitting from a sand trap into the wind, wear a hat, keep your head down, close your mouth and shut your eyes immediately after impact.
2. Use one club difference in your play for every 10 MPH of wind velocity against or with you. A normal 5 iron shot becomes a 6 iron shot with the wind and a 4 iron against it.

3. When hitting into the wind, don't swing hard. Play the ball back in your normal stance, use a less lofted club, if your hitting a driver, grip down slightly, and tee the ball lower. Slow your back swing down and take less than a full back swing but complete the swing to a full follow-through. This is called a *Knock-Down* shot. A solid struck ball will travel low and into the wind in an effort to achieve less wind resistance and greater distance. Also known as a *Wind-Cheater*

4. General rule when driving or hitting into a cross wind is to hit a shot that will "ride" the wind.

PLAYING IN THE RAIN

Normally you wouldn't purposely play in the rain, except for really exceptional avid golfers like those who read this book. Always carry an umbrella (usually with the biggest spread possible), a rain suit just in case, several dry towels, and at least three dry gloves. Wear appropriate clothing especially a wide brim hat and shoes that are water proof.

"The only thing I fear on a golf course is lightening – and Ben Hogan."
Sam Snead[16]

Bob Hope: *"If I'm on the course and lightning starts, I get inside fast. If God wants to play through, let him."*

When playing in the rain:

1. Wet greens hold better and roll slower, so aim at the top of the pin instead of the bottom to insure you get to the hole. When hitting to the green, loft is the key.

2. Don't over swing. Use your normal swing tempo to a full follow-through.

3. Check the putting surface for standing water. It will take a harder putt to get through the water.

PLAYING IN EXTREME COLD

Not many people, who live in areas that have snow, play golf in the winter months. But there are people like you and me that do. So here are my thoughts about that: Good for you! Don't let a few solid rain drops stop you from having fun playing a relaxing game of golf, especially if it is the only day you get to play.

Playing in cold weather off frozen ground and hitting to hard greens takes a little more knowledge and skill to be able to score well. It is well advised to practice a lot of chipping and pitching at home for that is where you are going to gain or loose a lot of strokes.

Playing in cold weather also calls for some adjustments in technique and strategy. Cold weather dictates that you warm up and stretch more than usual before playing. In particular, stretch the back muscles to allow a full turn. When wearing a lot of clothing, your swing will be hampered and will require shortening. Simple swing within limits and use one more club for normal distance shots or one less club for more roll to the green. You should shorten your back swing but always try to complete a full follow-through.

Your going to be hitting from hard ground so don't try to take a divot. Play the ball back in your stance and swing shallow. Distance is not going to be the biggest problem control is, so keep your ball in play with shorter shots.

Use a ball with a low compression during cold weather. It will be easier to compress and more controllable. Always play short of the green, allowing for the ball roll on the hard surface.

CHAPTER XVI

"Beginnings of Golf Club Making"

"Borrrrinnng"

For those golfers who find this book interesting either because it was somewhat humorous, entertaining, and even enlightening will probably want to quit reading now unless you find golf history fascinating and would like to learn about how golf clubs evolved as did the golf club makers. Sorry, not much humor here, but it is interesting and has a wealth of knowledge about golf clubs and their humble beginnings.

For the most part, this information came from the book "The Modern Guide to Golf Clubmaking" by Tom Wishon written for the Dynacraft Golf Products, Inc. in Newark, Ohio, copyright 1991.

"In the Beginning, God created…"

Golf, regardless of whether it were the Dutch, the Romans, the Italians, French, English or the Scots who were credited for the game of golf, the fact remains that clubs and balls were required for participation. While it is thought that Roman *paganica* players often used just common sticks or even Sheppard's crooks as their "clubs," each of the ensuing games that resembled golf called for a striking implement specially fashioned by skilled individuals for the purpose of playing the game.

As a result, golf club making has to be considered as old as the game itself. Ian Henderson and David Stirk, in their 1981 historical treatise, *Golf in the Making*, stated that the first written account of golf clubmaking could be traced to a record of purchase of golf clubs for King James IV of Scotland in the year 1502.

In their research the British authors found that many of the early clubmakers were, in fact, bowmakers. Due to gunpowder and firearms displacing the bow and arrow as the weapon of choice many bowmakers turned to golf clubmaking as a "*sideline*" business. As golf evolved and more and more people began to participate in the game, the role of full-time clubmakers soon became established. Henderson and Stirk found references to individuals in the early 1600s who were appointed as official clubmakers to members of the royal family. Their research also showed that a number of full-time clubmakers became established throughout the latter half of the 17th century in several Scottish towns where the game enjoyed exceptional popularity.

The oldest set of golf clubs in existence today date to the late 1600s, a set accidentally discovered behind a wall during the renovation of an old Scottish house. This set is on display in the clubhouse of the Royal Troon G.C. affording us a glimpse of early clubmaking design and workmanship. As these and other antique clubs are retrieved, there comes a clearer picture of not only who the first full-time professional clubmakers were, but how their clubs and skills changed and evolved over the years.

To some, the names Cossack, Philip, Forgan, McEwan, Morris, Dunn, Park and Patrick are recognizable as a few of the "fathers of clubmaking." Prior to the late 1700s, most clubmakers operated as one-man or small family businesses. As the family clubmaking firms expanded, so did the paths of distribution of the clubs they produced. In the late 1800s some of the firms began to branch out and deliver orders for clubs to other communities in "retail outlets."

Because many early clubmaking firms were headed and staffed by golf professionals, many new designs and models began to appear. The clubmaking professionals of the time would utilize their playing ability and golfing imagination to come up with new ideas for clubs in an attempt to develop better equipment and establish superiority over the other practitioners of the trade. In fact, so creative were some of their designs that many of the clubmaking innovations of the 1800s have been "reintroduced" by modern club manufacturers in the second half of the 20th century. As an example of this practice of reintroduction, the Stan Thompson Company's runner sole Ginty wood, thought by most upon its introduction in the 1970s to be a completely new design, in fact owes its origin to runner sole wood called the Tom Ball Altus Spoon...made in the late 1890's.

From their research for *Golf in the Making*, Henderson and Stirk found written reference to shaftmaking as early as 1687, from an entry in the diary of one Thomas Kincaid of Edinbourgh that noted hazelwood was used by clubmakers to produce shafts. Another common hardwood used for producing early wood shafts was ash. Readily available in England and Scotland, ash had been used for centuries for making drawbows. In addition, some clubmakers used lemonheart (lemonwood), greenheart, and lancewood for shaft making, but while able to resist warping better than ash, these hardwoods were higher in density and tended to result in shafts that were much stiffer and heavier that what was considered standard at the time.

In the mid 1800's America began to export hickory to Britain for use as handles for axes and other various hand tools. Hickory was not native to England and Scotland, and when clubmakers experimented with the wood, they found that the strength and flexibility characteristics of hickory were better suited for making shafts than hazelwood and ash. The British clubmakers' demand for hickory shafts increased heavily over the 1800s and it was not long before the exporting American firms began to switch from simply shipping the logs and pre-cut billets to taking over entire process of manufacturing of the finished shafts.

This was a significant step in the evolution of clubmaking for it not only took the time consuming step of actual shaft making out of the hands of the clubmakers, but it established an important domestic supply source for America's later entry into the golf club manufacturing industry.

The predominant set makeup in the 17th, 18th and early 19th centuries consisted almost entirely of wooden headed clubs. The hand stitched "featherie" was the predominant ball of the time, but was fragile and tended to break apart when struck by a heavy headed iron club. As a result, very few irons were produced and early clubmakers developed and practiced the skills of woodmaking only. Clubmakers had to cut their own hardwoods and make each individual head by hand. Other hardwoods were then introduced such as apple, pear and thorn to handle the feather golf ball.

When balls made from gutta percha displaced the "featherie" in the middle 1800s, new clubhead materials had to be found. The "gutty" was more durable and performed better than the feather ball, but it was much harder and had a tendency to chip and crack clubheads made from apple or pear. As a result, clubmakers began using beech, a wood that was in plentiful supply in Britain. Beech became popular for clubmaking because it was less brittle than previously used woodhead materials and possessed a natural resilience that could better withstand the stress of impact with the harder gutta percha ball.

As mentioned earlier, because of the adverse effects they had on the leather covered feather ball, very few iron-headed golf clubs were produced. Small headed "rut irons" were carried by some golfers to extricate a ball from a wagon wheel track, and a number of other assorted irons existed for general play when there was a question on a particular shot whether the wooden head would be damaged if used.

Because working with metal was not one of the skills possessed by early clubmakers, early ironheads were hand forged by local blacksmiths and then dispatched to the clubmaker for assembly with the shaft and grip. Because the term "clubmaker" applied to the craftsman who produced only woods, the ironhead makers became a separate entity known as "cleekmakers". When the gutta percha ball replaced the featherie, irons began to gain in popularity. Full time cleekmaking shops opened and golfers soon became used to frequenting both the clubmaker's and the cleekmaker's establishments to acquire their full set of clubs.

"COMING TO AMERICA…"

At the same time that clubmaking in Britain was progressing by leaps and bounds. America was just beginning to discover the game of golf. Commercial travel across the Atlantic Ocean was becoming more commonplace, and some American businessmen traveling abroad had the opportunity to become introduced to the game. Upon their return to the States, the newfound interest they had acquired in golf coupled with the previous golfing experience of British émmigrés introduced golf to America. What started in New York with "The Apple Tree Gang" in 1888 soon began to boom and by 1900 there were an estimated 1,000 golf courses in the United States! Along with increased participation came a growing demand for instruction and equipment, so the first American clubmakers were actually English and Scottish professionals who had chosen to move abroad to take advantage of a new boom in U.S. golf.

Spalding first began producing golf clubs in 1894. Key to their entry into the clubmaking business was their ability to incorporate existing modern industrial methods into producing clubheads. Spalding was able to incorporate copy lathes in their facility for rough turning woodheads. Spalding is credited with being the first manufacturer to use large, drop hammers for the purpose of mass-producing raw iron heads. With this advance in the field of club manufacture, Spalding soon positioned itself as one of the largest manufactures of golf clubs in the world.

Equally important was the contribution of the other major American manufacturing concerns such as the Crawford McGregor & Canby Company of Dayton, Ohio. Although different versions of the story are in existence, its introduction of an all-new woodhead material further contributed to establishing American control of clubmaking. In a story that certainly must go down in the annals of golf, one day company head W.H. Crawford cracked the head of one of his woods. Not wanting to wait for a replacement from Scotland, he turned to his wooden shoe making company to correct the situation. George Mattern, a company engineer, fashioned a replacement from the wood used to make shoes. This hardwood was called persimmon and was tougher than the beech being used in existing clubheads, and in Mattern's opinion would make a superior head for overcoming the stress of impact between the clubhead and ball.

Just 12 years after the game of golf was introduced to the United States, America had 1,000 courses. By 1910, there were 1,400 golf courses, and by 1931 the number of golf facilities swelled to nearly 5,000! Unbelievably, between 1910 and 1930 the number of American golfers literally exploded, growing from 350,000 to 2,000,000! Golf was the sport of the day and there was just no way the clubmaking industry's pre-1900 was of conducting business could survive in the face of such increases.

In 1910 in Newark, Ohio, the Burke Golf Shaft Company decided to expand its production and began to produce complete golf clubs to complement its already existing hickory shaft making venture.

The Thomas E Wilson Company of Chicago, through an existing sporting goods manufacturing division, expanded into clubmaking in 1914, and in 1916 The Hillerich and Bradsby Company branched out from the baseball bat business to go into clubmaking. Because many club professionals in America had developed club repair and assembly skills from their British roots, each of the American clubmaking companies continued to sell clubheads and component parts in addition to their fully-manufactured clubs. With so many supply sources manufacturing and selling finished component parts, the professionals no longer need to practice their full clubmaking skills, but could still "custom assemble" golf clubs made from component parts for their golfing members. Thus, the foundation for the practice of today's custom clubmakers to custom build golf clubs from component parts was established many years ago.

<u>GETTING FROM THERE TO HERE</u>

Perhaps the greatest clubmaking controversy of the early 20th century concerned the golf industry's switch from hickory shafts to steel shafts. Hickory shaft suppliers and the clubmakers who were faithful to the wooden shafts seized on the poor quality of the first metal shafts to convince golfers that steel shafts were not only deficient to wood in performance, but were bad for the game. American clubmaking companies, more concerned with improving the quality of equipment than preserving the traditional nature of the game, moved much faster than their British counterparts to accept the shafts. The controversy started with a little known patent for a steel shaft design in 1894 did not end until 1931, when Billy Burke won the U.S. Open and became the last player to win a major tournament using hickory shafts.

As with any manufacturing oriented field, the technical advances of component parts and clubmaking techniques are what have been responsible for the constant improvement of the quality of golf clubs. The list of technical achievements in clubmaking is almost endless. When machinery entered the clubmaking shop, more clubs could be produced and done so at a lower price; therefore, more golfers could in turn gain access to the game. After steel shafts had replaced hickory, golfers no longer have to worry about shaft durability, inconsistency or poor shot results due to excess torsion. Step tapering of shafts allowed more precise playability differences from shaft to shaft. The *Laird Shaft*, a type of steel shaft seen in clubs produced circa 1900, was a solid shaft with numerous holes drilled in it to reduce weight. These clubs are highly prized by collectors.

The next step was introduction of the sole plate to the wooden heads to prevent wear and tear on the bottom of the head. Entirely by accident, the clubhead's performance was improved due to the fact that the center of gravity of the head was lowered in the process. The effect such a change could have on shot performance was not understood by clubmakers or golfers for years after the alteration; all they knew at the time was that for some reason, the "Brassies" could produce more successful shots from slightly questionable lie conditions than clubs without the metal plate on the sole.

After WWII, giant milling machines produced more intricate shapes into the back of irons allowing club designers the ability to "re-distribute" weight on the back of the head. Drilling machines were adapted for drilling iron hosels allowing further weight control for iron heads.

As golf moved into its next great boom period, "The Palmer Era," the technology of the industry was well established but the technological awareness of the golf was not. Golfers still selected clubs on the basis of what the current stars of the day used and not with regard for what might be best suited to them. Then in what could be arguably be termed the most significant clubmaking breakthrough in the history of golf, the public began to achieve an awareness of equipment technology that began to force golf club manufacturers to offer more scientifically-proven game improvement designs.

That breakthrough was the advent of investment casting as a method of producing wood and iron clubheads. With investment casting, foundries could supply manufactures with an entirely new array of design shapes. Deep back cavities were now possible and the look of an ironhead was only limited by the imagination of the designers. The terms perimeter weighting and center of gravity became household words for golfers.

Now we have the metal wood heads, as big a "melons" and graphite shafts lighter than hickory and stronger than steel. Ah progress, don't you just love it? Clubmakers today enjoy the capability of performing any type of repair or custom fitting due to the advances in the technology of clubmaking by the component companies. New epoxies that set in 2 to 30 minutes allow us to build a club and use it in a hours time. New shafts allow for shot control by providing a wide variation of flexes, kick points, weights, and torques.

With the new graphite shafts, the overall club weight can be reduced drastically and provides a shock absorber for the impact shock caused by ball or ground impact during the swing. Graphite shafts also provide added shaft flexibility and club head speeds. The latest innovation in golf club shafts built and distributed exclusively by Wilson Golf is the new "Half –and-Half" shaft with the new line of D-Fy irons and hybrids. This shaft is steel from the head to a mid-shaft point then turn into graphite through the butt of the club. Great feel and club head control.

Then there is the new grips…. well that's the rest of the story told below.

<u>ORIGIN OF THE GRIP</u>

In the early days of clubmaking, golf clubs were not made with a grip. Since shafts were all hand made, 17th century clubmakers would simply shape the butt end of the shaft larger in diameter to accommodate a golfer's hands. However, because the game was often played under wet conditions, and because of the uncomfortable vibration felt in the hands from the shock of impact, clubmakers began the practice of wrapping strips of leather and sheepskin on the end of the shaft to solve the problems. The first grips were large in diameter, which coincided with the accepted instructional technique of the time to grip the club more in the palms than in the fingers. To produce larger diameter grips, strips of wool or linen were wrapped under the leather or sheepskin grip. Wool strips often came from the ends of bolts of wool, called the rind of the fabric, while the linen strips became known as "listings." Because these strips were used under the leather, the term "underlisting" was adopted and is still used today to refer to the foundation of leather grips.

Through the era of the gutta percha golf ball, grips remained large to help absorb what was an even more harsh vibration that was felt from impact with this very hard ball. The size of the grips began to decrease in the 20th century with the more resilient rubber core ball. This required thinner underlistings and as wood shafts turned to steel shafts in the 1920's paper replaced fabric for the purpose of creating the foundation for leather grips. Leather wrapped grips eventually gave way to the rubber and leather slip-on grips and the underlistings became masking and two sided tape.

References

1 "And then Jack said to Arnie..." by Don Wade, CB Contemporary Books, Chicago, Ill 1991

2 "The Modern Guide to Golf Clubmaking" by Tom Wishon, A Dynacraft® Publication, Newark, Ohio 1991

3 "The Handbook of Golf" by Alex Hay

4 The PGA Manual of Golf, The professional Way to Play Better GOLF, Gary Wiren, PH.D., MacMillian Publishing Company. New York, New York, 1991.

5 Golf Digest Magazine, June 1993

6 The Official EXCEPTIONS to the Rules of Golf, Henry Beard, John Boswell Associates Book, Villard Books, New York, New York, 1992

7 Bits & Pieces magazine, Lawrence Ragan Communications, Inc. Chicago, IL

8 United States Golf Association "The Rules of Golf" booklet effective January 1, 2004

9 A quote from Leslie Nelson from his video "Bad Golf Made Easier", Capital Cities/ABC Video Publishing Inc. Standford, CT.

10 "The Golfer's Stroke-Saving Handbook" by Craig Shankland, Dale Shankland, Dom Lupo and Roy Benjamin, Harper Perennial, New York, New York, 1978

11 "Playing the Great Game of Golf" by Ken Blanchard, William Morrow and Company, Inc, New York, New York, 1992

12 "The Why Book of Golf" by William C. Koren, Price Stern Sloan, Los Angeles, California 1992

13 Golf Journal Magazine, The Official Publication of the United States Golf Association. 1994

14 GOLF Magazine, Article by Jeff Rude "A Little Action," February, 1995 issue.

15 "GOLF Magazine's TIPS from the Teaching Pros" by the Editors of GOLF Magazine, Harper & Row Publishers, New York, New York, 1969

16 The Golf Joke Book by Bob Lonigan, Barnes & Noble, 1996

17 Senior Golfer Magazine, Jan/Feb 1994 issue, Article by John Olman.

18 "The Complete Golf Club Fitting Program" by Ralph Maltby, Ralph Maltby Enterprizes, Newark, Ohio, 1986

19 "The Best of Golf Digest, The First 25 Years" Golf Digest Inc, New York, New York, 1975

20 "Harvey Pennick's Little Red Book" by Harvey Pennick, Simon and Schuster, New York, New York, 1992

21 Author unknown. information taken from a research paper left in a library book and passed on to me by Dick Boan, a member of the Golf Collectors Society.

22 Golf Tips Magazine, issues from 1993 through 1994.

23 "Target Golf" by Roy Pace, Rudledge Books, a division of Sammis Publishing Corp., NY, NY\

24 Golf Pro Magazine, article by David Chmiel, May/June issue 1994.

25 "The inner Game of Golf" by W. Timothy Gallway, Random House Inc, NY, NY 1981

26 Golfsmith Clubmaker Magazine, Article by Paul Wattles, "Good Golf Vs Real Golf," August 1994

27 The Professional Clubmaker's Society Journal, Professional Club Maker's Society, Assistant Editor Stacy Taylor, Louisville, Kentucky, 1993 & 1994

28 "The Search for the Perfect Swing" by Alastair Cochran & John, The Booklegger, Grass Valley, CA. 1989.

29 Bits & Pieces magazine, Lawrence Ragan Communications, Inc. Chicago, IL

30 "The Golf Secrets of the BIG-MONEY Pros" by Jerry Heard, The Hanford Press 1992

31 "Golf Clubmaking and Repair" by Carl Paul, Published by Paul Associates, Austin, Texas 1984

GLOSSARY of GOLF TERMS

A

Abrade: The process of removing chrome finish from a steel shaft or the layer of paint from a graphite shaft prior to installation of the shaft into the head.

Accelerated Tip Response: Golf shaft technology, pioneered by UST, in which the tip of the shaft is more flexible than the rest of the shaft, creating a softer feel and potentially higher trajectory.

Acetone: Chemical used to bring ferrules to high luster as a final step in assembly.

Aerify: Process of boring small holes, typically less than ¾" in diameter, into the putting green (or fairway) in order to improve growth. Usually done twice a year, once in April and once in October.

Aernet: Patented high strength steel made by Carpenter Steel, used primarily as a face material for large volume stainless steel drivers.

Air Hammer: Mechanical device, typically run by an air compressor, that forces a shaft into a head under high pressure.

Albatross: A double eagle; a score of 3 under par on a hole.

Alloy: Any combination of metal used to produce a club head or shaft. Alloys may contain aluminum, steel, beryllium, nickel, copper, titanium, or any number of other metals in varying combinations.

Aluminum Oxide: Media used in sandblasting applications of metal wood heads and iron faces.

Aluminum Shafts: Golf shafts formed from aluminum tubing, used primarily in the 1960's and 70's.

Amateur: Any golfer who plays the game for enjoyment and who does not receive direct monetary compensation due to his or her playing or teaching skills.

Anti-Shank: General term given to older hickory shafted golf clubs that had large bends or offsets in their hosels to eliminate shanked shots.

Arc: The nearly circular curve around the body made by a golf swing.

Ascending Weight Technology: The concept of utilizing lighter shafts in the long irons of a set for added club head speed and distance, while using heavier shafts in the shorter irons to promote control.

Attihedral: Pattern of dimples on a ball comprised of four straight rows of dimples around the middle of the ball, with four around each pole. Small triangular arrays of dimples fill the remaining area on the ball. This creates 8 triangular groupings of dimples on the ball. This pattern may also be called octohedtral.

Autoclave: A pressured heating device used for shaft construction. The autoclave is a heat treating chamber which applies pressure and high temperature to a material in order to cure it.

B

Backscrew: Steel pin or screw used to help secure a steel shaft to a wooden head.

Balance Point: The point at which a shaft achieves equilibrium; the point at which a shaft's weight is evenly distributed in both directions when rested on a single fulcrum point.

Balata: Natural or synthetic compound used as a cover material for balls. Characterized by a soft feel and high spin rate. Less durable than other balls.

Belly Putter: Type of putter in which the butt of the grip is positioned against the player's stomach in order to create a pendulum effect. Most belly putters are about 40" in length. Popularized by Vijay Singh and Paul Azinger, among others on the PGA and Seniors PGA tours.

Beltronics (Beltronics Swingmate): Computerized device (approximately 4" X 6") for measuring swing speed.

Bent Grass: Type of grass. Characterized by thin blades, found on most courses with varying seasonal climates.

Bend Point: The point of maximum bending on a shaft as measured by a compression test of the shaft on both the tip and butt ends. Also known as the "kick point."

Bermuda Grass: Type of grass found on most courses located in warmer or tropical climates. Characterized by thick blades and "grainy" surface.

Big Butt Shaft: Any shaft with a butt size over .620" is considered to be a big butt shaft.

Big Butt Grip Installation Tool: An expandable plastic tool that helps to start the grip onto the butt of a large butt shaft. Taylor Made woods often have big butt shafts.

Bi-Metal: A club head constructed from two different materials. A common example is a stainless steel club head with a brass sole insert or brass sole rails.

Bi-Matrix Shaft: Patented by True Temper, the Bi-Matrix is a shaft that employs a graphite and steel section in the same shaft. Bi-Matrix wood shafts have a steel tip section, with the remainder being made of graphite.

Black Ice[TM]: A proprietary face coating applied to the face of a club in order to increase spin. Primarily used on wedges, but can be applied to woods, irons and putters also.

Blade Length: The measurement of an iron head from the radius of the crotch of the head to the farthest point of the toe.

Blade Height: The measurement of an iron head at the center of the face from the ground line to the top line.

Blind Bore: A bore configuration of metal woods in which the shaft penetrates the bore to a stand depth of ½" from the sole of the club head.

Bluing (Gun Bluing): Process of applying finish to un-plated carbon steel putters. The resulting finish is a deep blue color and resists rust.

Boring (Hosel Boring): The process, using a drill or drill press, of enlarging the hosel bore of a wood, iron or putter.

Bore-Through: A hosel type in which the shaft penetrates through the sole of the club. Callaway™ clubs are the best examples of bore-through heads.

Bore Type: The term used to describe how far a shaft penetrates into a club head's hosel.

Boron: A high strength element added to some graphite shafts to increase tip strength.

Bounce Sole Iron: An iron in which the trailing edge is lower than the leading edge.

Borrow: A term, mostly British, referring to how much break will need to be anticipated when lining up a putt

Boxed Set: Popular method of packaging beginner or junior sets found at larger retail stores. Boxed sets typically consists of 8 irons, 3 woods a putter and a bag for one low price.

Bramble: Type of ball, popular on the 1890's which featured a gutta-percha cover hand hammered into a series of constant surface textures or patterns.

Brazing: The proprietary bonding technology used by many companies in the golf industry to secure the club face to the head.

Bubble™ Shaft: A composite shaft, proprietary to Taylor Made, that is designed to stabilize the club head at impact. It features a recessed section just below the grip. It is also unique in that the butt diameter of the shaft is .800", requiring a special grip.

Build-Up Tape: Masking tape applied to the butt end of the shaft to increase grip size. A single layer of masking tape (.005" thick) will increase grip size about 1/64".

Bushing Ferrule: A type of ferrule that is used to reduce the size of a metal wood hosel to .335" from a larger diameter or to reduce an iron hosel to .370" from a larger diameter.

Butt Cap: The end of the grip of a golf club. Also called an **End Cap**.

Butt Diameter: The measure of the diameter of the larger end of a shaft, typically expressed in thousandths. (i.e., .600" or .580") Also **Butt Size**.

Butt Heavy: A type of shaft construction in which the butt section of the shaft is heavier than the equal length of the tip section. Most graphite and parallel tip shafts are considered to be butt heavy shafts.

Butt Trim: Term applied when cutting a shaft to the butt end.

Butt Weight: The process of adding weight (also called the Butt Weight) to the butt end of the shaft.

Buy.Com Tour: Male professional golf circuit, new in 2000, for players one level below the PGA Tour.

C

Caddie Master: A course employee responsible for managing caddies and assigning them to players as required.

Calipers: A measuring device commonly used to measure the diameters of grips and shafts.

Carpenter Steel: An alloy of steel produced by the Carpenter Company that is used to produce golf club heads. Has a higher strength-to-weight ratio than most stainless steels.

Carry-Double: A caddie employed by two players and who players and who typically carries two bags.

Cart Fee: Fee required to rent a riding golf cart for 9 or 18 holes.

Casting: (Lost Wax Investment Casting) The investment casting process used to produce irons, putters, and metal woods that initially involves making a master model of the club head. A mold is then made from the master. Wax is injected into these molds forming a duplicate of the club head. A ceramic material is then used to coat the waxes. The ceramic is heated after hardening causing the wax to be removed. Metal is then poured into the now empty ceramic pieces to form the actual investment cast club head.

Center of Gravity (CG): The point in a club head at which all of the points of balance intersect. Lower CG higher the ball flight.

Center-Shafted: A type of hosel configuration, common in putters, in which the shaft enters the head toward the center. Bullseye-type putters are the best known examples of center-shafted putters.

Ceramic Fiber: A series of man-made ceramic materials that may be used in shaft or head manufacture.

Chamfer: Generic term used to describe the process of using a special tool to "countersink", "radius" or "cone" the inside of a hosel in order to help provide a measure of protection, particularly for a graphite shaft.

Channel Back: Also known as "undercut", a club design in which a channel or cavity is created through the addition of weight along the back cavity of a club. These club designs move the CG of the club rearward, making it easier to get the ball airborne.

Chili Dip: A shot is which a player hits behind the ball, not moving it very far. May also be referred to as a "fat" shot or a "chunk".

Chip Out: A shot, generally going only a short distance, made from trouble in an attempt to get the ball back in play.

Chop Saw: A motorized saw used in larger shops to cut numerous shafts at one time.

Chrome Plated Finish: Type of finish electrostatic ally applied to forged irons.

Clean and Dip: Process of using steel wool or light sandpaper on a wood head followed by the application of a coat of polyurethane in order to bring the club back to a "shiny" finish.

Cleek Mark: The mark on the back of a hickory shafted club that helps to identify the maker of the club.

Coefficient of Restitution (COR): The amount of energy put into a golf ball as compared to the amount of energy at (after) impact. The COR is the relation between rebound velocity and initial velocity.

Component: Any of the parts used to assembly golf clubs, be they heads, shafts, or grips.

Compression: The deflection a ball undergoes under a compressive load. Loosely defined as the hardness of the ball. Identified by the number color and a number, a higher number (i.e. 100) indicates a ball that requires more force to compress it. 100 compression ball is normally identified with black numbers.

Compression Molded: A manufacturing method for graphite heads and face inserts in which layers of graphite are placed upon one another and heat cured to create the club head or insert.

Course Rating: A numerical rating, usually by a recognized organization such as the USGA, that identifies the difficulty of a course. For example, a course rated 72.4 is more difficult than one rated at 68.5. A scratch player should be expected to shoot a 68 or 69 on the course rated 68.5.

CNC (Computer Numerically Controlled) Milling: A production method, usually used for putters, in which the entire head is milled from a soft block of stainless steel. A computer controls the milling machine.

Cone: Generic term used to describe the process of using a special tool to "countersink" or "radius" the inside of a hosel in order to help provide a measure of protection, particularly for a graphite shaft.

Conforming Club: A golf club whose construction permits it to be used in events as sanctioned by the USGA.

Conforming Ball: Any golf ball that is permitted for tournament use under the USGA Rules of Golf as detailed in Rule Book Appendix II.

Constant Weight: A shafting concept in which all of the shafts in a given set weigh the same.

Core (*Ball*): Any one of various material used inside the golf ball. A solid core ball utilizes a hard material inside the cover, a wound core ball typically has a softer core covered by a series of windings and the cover.

Core (Grip): The inside diameter measurement of a grip. Typically core sizes match shaft butt size. For example, an M60 grip core will match with a .600" shaft butt size and produce a standard grip size.

Counter Balance: The process of adding weight in the butt end of a shaft to achieve a specific swing weight and /or feel. Counter balancing will increase the overall weight of the club and is not a widely recommended procedure.

Countersink: The process of using a special tool to radius the inside of a hosel in order to help provide a measure of protection, particularly for a graphite shaft. The term may also be used to describe the tool used to create the countersink.

Crimp: The mechanical process of "punching" two or more places on a shaft tip in order to make it fit more securely into a hosel.

Cryogenics: Branch of science dealing with the freezing of an object to alter its physical properties. Used to treat club heads, cryogenics aligns the molecules in the head material for a harder, more durable product.

CTU: Cast Thermoset Technology used by Callaway Golf in the development of their line of golf balls.

Cubic Centimeters (*cc's*): The units used to measure the volume of a wood head. The measurement is generally made as a water displacement test whereby a wood head is immersed in water and the amount of water displaced in the head's volume.

Curved Shaft: A shaft, usually steel or aluminum, designed for use in no-hosel putters, that features and or bends no more than 5" from the shaft tip. The curved shaft tends to create offset and possible face balancing on putters with no hosel.

Cushion Shaft: Designed and used by Ping as a vibration ampening piece in their Cushion Shafts. The Cushion consists of a rubbery material encasing three ball bearings. It is inserted inside the shaft below the grip.

Cycles Per Minute (*CPM*): The common measurement units discussing the frequency of a shaft.

D

Darrell Survey: Organization that counts and publishes equipment usage on professional golf tours. The Survey counts club and ball type and brand, type of clothing and shoes used, etc.

Deburr: Process of removing any rough edges or surfaces from the inside of a hosel or from the inside of a shaft prior to installing a shaft into a head.

Deep Bore: A model of wood or iron whose hosel bore depth exceeds 1 1/2 ".

Deflection: The comparative measure of the relative stiffness of a shaft as measured by securing a weight toward the tip of a shaft (club) and relating this to a known stiffness scale.

Deep Face: A club face that measures higher than average from the sole of the club top the crown.

Deltahedral: Dimple pattern on a ball characterized by 24 triangular rows of dimples.

Determinator: A patented device invented by True Temper to measure how a player "loads" a shaft. The readings from the Determinator are then used in recommending a True Temper shaft.

Diamond Face: Popularized by the Purespin™ Golf Company, a face coating utilizing fine diamond crystals to produce more backspin and a longer wearing face surface.

Die Cast: Process of club head production (primarily used with zinc or aluminum) in which heads are formed through the injection of material into a pre-formed die.

Discrete Flex: A shaft having a specific flex design. For example, True Temper's Dynamic Gold™ S300 is a discrete flex shaft, while the company's parallel tipped Dynamic Gold™ shaft is not.

Distance Standard: USGA parameter for conforming balls that limits their overall carry and roll to 280 yards or less (+/-6%).

DMC: Proprietary grip compound, characterized by its soft feel, developed by the Lampkin Grip Corporation.

Dodecahedral: Dimple pattern that arranges the dimples into 12 pentagonal arrays.

Dot Punch: A series of circular indentations or dots on the face of an iron head (mostly wedges) in place of lines.

Double-Cover Ball: A ball with a large central core surrounded by two thinner materials, one of them being the cover. The purpose of the additional cover is to add spin on shorter shots for control and to reduce spin on longer shots for distance.

Double-Sided Tape: Also known as "two way tape" or "grip tape", special tape (3/4" or 2" wide) that is adhesive on both sides.

Drag: Wind resistance as a golf ball flies.

Driving Plug: Steel rod, with a recessed section, slightly smaller than a shaft butt, placed into the shaft butt and then struck with a hammer in order to seat the shaft to the bottom of the hosel when assembling a club.

Droop (Shaft Droop): The movement of a club head, toe down, as caused by the club being swung and the shaft bending perpendicular to the ground line.

Dynacraft Shaft Fitting Index: The industries first "apples-to-apples" method of shaft classification.

Dynamic Fitting: The preferred method of fitting in which the golfer undertakes a series of fitting tests while actually hitting balls.

E

Easy Out: Threaded steel rod inserted into a shaft broken off at the hosel. The threads lock onto the shaft, making it removable after the application of heat. Also called a "shaft extractor."

Electric Screw Extractor: A tool with two electrically charged electrodes that, when placed in contact with a soleplate or face insert screw, makes the screw easier to remove due to its heat melting the epoxy holding the screw in place.

Elastomer™: Material used in the formation of golf balls, particularly by Titleist™. Also, a variety of material used in the manufacturing of Winn™ grips.

Elastomer™ Ring: A piece of polymer material used to surround the inner cavity of certain models of irons, notably Lynx Black Cat™ models. The ring is used for cosmetic and acoustic purposes according to Lynx.

Emery Cake: Type of compound used, along with an unstitched buffing wheel, to remove deep nicks and scratches from a steel surface.

Epoxy: Two-part adhesive used to secure golf shafts to heads.

E.R.C.: The most famous of the non-conforming flexible-face drivers. Manufactured by Callaway Golf, E.R.C. are the initials of the company's founder, Ely Reese Callaway.

Extending Shafts: The process of using a piece of material inserted into the shaft to make the club longer.

F

Face Balanced: A putter that, when balanced toward the shaft tip, will exhibit the property of the putter face being parallel to the ground line.

Face Centerline: An imaginary line intersecting the center of the club face.

Face insert: The center portion of he face on a wooden, composite, or metal head, typically constructed from epoxy, graphite, or some type of fibrous material. Effective with a 1992 USGA ruling, all types of woods, irons and putters may have face inserts.

Face progression: The measurement from a shaft's centerline to the front of the club face.

Face Radius Gauge: Four-sided gauge used to measure the bulge and roll of a club face.

Face Screw: Aluminum, brass or steel screws used to help secure face inserts into wooden or graphite wood heads.

Fairway Metal: Generic term applied to any metal wood used from the fairway.

Fancy Face: Generic term given to antique wooden woods whose faces featured unusual designs, usually constructed from different materials.

Fat Shaft™: A shaft, designed by Wilson, that utilizes an oversized tip, over-hosel design in an attempt to provide head/shaft stabilization on off-center hits.

Fiber (Fibre): Material, usually comprised of layers of a paper or phenolic material used to make inserts for wooden woods.

Filament Winding: A method of composite shaft manufacture in which a continuous strand of material (typically graphite fiber) is wrapped around a mandrel to create a shaft. Filament wound shafts are often a bit more consistent than sheet wrapped models.

Fire Forged: Term given to the forging of a titanium wood head (particularly its face) under extremely high temperatures.

Fit Chip: Computerized device attached to the shaft of a club that establishes the proper frequency of shaft for a given player. Used along with a computer during clubmaker shaft fitting.

Fitting Chart: Generic term applied to any number of club demo programs that include some type of cart allowing clubs to easily carried to and displayed on the range during a fitting.

Flare™ **Tip Shaft**: A composite shaft characterized by a tip diameter of +/- .440" at the point it enters the hosel. Originally designed by Unifiber for the Lynx Black Cat™ golf club, the design theory behind this shaft is head stabilization at impact.

Flat Lie: The term given to an iron or a wood having a lie flatter than specification. For example. If the spec is 60 degrees, a 2 degree flat club would have a lie angle of 58 degrees.

Flat Line Frequency: A method of frequency matching in which all of the woods or irons in the set maintain the same frequency. When plotted on a graph, the frequencies appear as a straight line.

Flat Line Oscillation (FLO): Process of making all of the shafts in a set of clubs the same frequency, either in raw or assembled form.

Flexable Face: The face of a golf club, typically constructed of some type of forged titanium, that is designed to "flex" upon ball impact, thus potentially propelling the ball a longer distance than if the face did not flex.

Flow Weighting: A method of head design in which the positioning of the weight in the head moves across the head from one club to the next. For example, a #1 iron may have more weight concentrated on its toe, a #2 iron slightly less, and so on.

Forged Face: Typical of titanium woods, the process of forging a specific material for use in the face. The material may be an alloy of titanium such as 15-3-3-3 or SP700, to name two.

Form Forged: Iron-production process in which a head is first cast and is then forged to create its final shape. The forging aligns the grain structure of the head, the initial casting makes the process more cost effective.

48" Ruler: Aluminum ruler used to measure raw lengths of shafts and total length of golf clubs when they are held in their playing position.

Fried Egg: Lie in a sand bunker in which most of the ball in below the surface of the sand. Visually, the ball looks like a "fried egg", hence the term.

Forged Titanium: A method of wood head manufacture in which the body and sole of head is formed (forged) from 100% (pure) titanium. The face and hosels of such woods are cast from 6-4 ti. Forged titanium woods are less costly due to their ease of forming as well as their lower raw material cost.

Forging: The process of producing a golf club in which the head is made from a series of forging dies stamping the head to final shape. Forged heads are made of softer metals than are cast heads and required laborious hand finishing and chrome plating in order to produce a finished product.

Four Way Radius: The sole design of an iron or wood in which there is a measurable radius of the sole both from heal to toe and from trailing edge to leading edge.

Frequency: The number of oscillations of a golf shaft in a given time when the tip is pulled down and the shaft vibrates I a specialized machine.

Frequency Analyzer: Specialized machine used to measure the frequencies of golf clubs and shafts. Used in the frequency matching process.

Frequency Matching: The process of ensuring that all of the clubs in a given set are matched by their shaft frequency. Frequency matched clubs are said to be more consistent in both feel and performance.

Frequency Slope: The graph line formed when plotting the frequency of the shafts in a set of clubs. A well-matched set will have a consistent slope; a mismatched set will show shafts that vary several cycles from their expected range.

Frequed: A slang term for the frequency matching of shafts.

G

Gear Effect: The effect, caused by face bulge, that tends to cause a ball hit toward the toe or heel side of face center to curve back to the intended target line.

GHIN: Golf Handicap Information Network.

Glanz Wach (Wax): Compound used along with a buffing wheel to create a high luster finish on a polyurethane coated wood or metal wood.

Gooseneck: General term given to a putter (or iron) that has an extremely offset hosel.

Gorse: Very thick grass and or/or shrubs from which it may be impossible to play a shot. Gorse is common on European seaside courses.

Grain: Direction of growth of blades of grass. Particularly noticeable on putting greens, the grain will have an influence on the direction and speed of the ball as it rolls.

Graphite: A synthetic material used for shaft and head production.

Graphite Shaft Remover (Extractor): Generic term given to any one of a number of tools designed to remove a graphite shaft from a steel or titanium head without damaging either the head or shaft.

Grip Collar: Plastic collar used to secure the bottom of a leather or Winn grip in place on the shaft.

Grip Core: The internal diameter of a grip as measured in thousandths. .600" is a M60.

Grip Gauge: Aluminum or plastic gauge used to determine a shaft or grip diameter.

Grip Mouth: The opening at the small end of the grip.

Grip Rip: Tool used to quickly remove a grip.

Grit Edge Blade: Type of blade installed in a hacksaw that is used to cut graphite shafts without splintering them.

Ground Line: The term given to the flat surface on which a club head is placed to measure its specifications. It is the line running from the club face to back, perpendicular to the shaft centerline. Ground line may be loosely interpreted to mean the position the club is placed in on the ground as the player address a shot on the course as well.

Gunmetal: Dark, almost black, finish applied to the surface of iron heads for either cosmetic reasons or to prevent rusting of a carbon steel head.

H

Hanging Lie: A ball resting on a uphill slope;

Hardpan: Term given to an area of the golf course (not bunkers or hazards) on which no grass if growing.

Heat Gun: Electrical device producing a flow of heated air that is used to break the epoxy bond between the graphite shaft and the club head's hosel.

Heating (Hot) Rod: Steel rod, usually with a wooden handle, that is heated and then inserted into a club's hosel in order to break the epoxy bond between the head and the shaft. Heating rod can be electrically heated or heated by blow torch.

Heel-Weighted: A golf club , typically an iron, featuring a high concentration of weight toward the heel.

Heel-Toe Weighting: A type of club head design in which weight is positioned toward the heel and toe of the club head in an attempt to stabilize the club head on off center shots.

High COR (HI-COR): A driver that has a coefficient of Restitution (COR) approaching or exceeding the USGA conforming limit of .83.

High Launch: A shaft that is designed with a flexible tip to assist a player in getting the ball into the air. Also a term used for balls that are designed for high, initial launch trajectory.

High-Modulus Graphite: A shaft material stiffer than standard graphite. The higher the modulus of graphite, the lower its compression strength.

High Polish Finish: Shiny (mirror) finish applied to stainless steel iron heads through a series of polishing belt operations.

HIP Steel: Hot Isostatic Process. Propietary stainless steel

characterized by soft feel and high tensile strength used by Orlimar and made popular in their driver line.

Hollow Iron: An iron head design that is made in two pieces. A Hollow iron is rather bulbous in shape; the design concept is to move the CG away from the face to help get the ball airborne. Hollow irons have perimeter weighting similar to smaller metal woods as well.

Home Green: The 18th green, or any other designated as the last to be played.

Hook Face: A wood that has a face angle that is closed. Hook face woods may help players who slice to hit the ball straight.

Horizontal Flow Weighting: A manner of distributing weight from club to club in a set of irons in which the highest concentration of weight moves from the toe of the longer irons to the heel of the shorter irons.

Hosel Adapter: Generic term applied to any type of bushing or replacement hosel for a wood or an iron. The hosel adapter reduces the size of the hosel opening so that a smaller diameter shaft can be installed. Special hosel adapters can also take the place of the Thermoplastic hosel of Ping drivers when reshafting them.

Hosel Boring: The process of enlarging a hosel bore through drilling.

Hosel Rivet: Aluminum or steel rivet (pin) used in certain models of irons (most notable Hogans, First Flights, and Older MacGregors) to help secure the shaft in place.

Hump Shaft™: Developed by Apollo Golf to move the balance point of the shaft toward the tip. This shaft is identified by a noticeable enlarged area directly above the hosel, extending approximately 5" up the shaft. The shaft is available in both steel and graphite.

I

In-Hosel: The common shaft-to-head installation in which the shaft penetrates into the hosel.

Initiation: Fee paid, up-front, prior to joining a private club. An initiation fee may vary between a few hundred dollars to nearly $100,000 at some of the most elite clubs in the world.

Injection Molding: A method of manufacture (typically involving wood heads and face inserts) in which the material (ABS, epoxy, graphite, etc.) comprising the head is heated to a liquid state and injected under pressure into a mold. When the material hardens, it takes the shape of the mold into which it was injected.

Insert Hosel: A club design which moves the position of the hosel toward the center of the club face in an attempt to reduce head twisting. The USGA Rule lists a maximum inset of .625" or 16 millimeters above the horizontal plane on which the club is resting in its normal address position.

Inverted Core Technology: Patented by TaylorMade, this echnology is used to create a driver face that possesses a high COR. The back of the face actually has a "cone-shaped" central area that increases the COR or the face according to TaylorMade

Iron Byron: Device that simulates the swing of a golfer (Byron Nelson) used by the USGA and major equipment companies for the testing of golf clubs and balls.

J

Jumbo Wood Head: A metal or wooden head having a volume of 250CC or more.

K

Keel Sole: The sole of a wooden club or metal wood that is "V" shaped and designed to lower the clubs CG to assist in getting the ball airborne from a less perfect lie.

Kevlar: A synthetic fiber manufactured by DuPont™ used in shaft and head production. It is known for its high energy absorbing characteristics, but is a lower modulus material and has limited compression properties.

Knurling: Decorative engraving or stamping on the hosel of an iron club.

L

Lag (Shaft Lag): Situation in which the club head lags behind the shaft toward impact as a result of the natural flexion of the shaft.

Large Butt Shaft: Any shaft with a butt size of over .620".

Launch Monitor: Computerized fitting unit used to determine the optimum drive loft for a given player through a series of high tests.

Leading Edge: The forward most point of the club face.

Lead Powder: Material used to swingweight steel-shafted clubs after shaft installation, but prior to grip installation. The powder is poured into the shaft to the hosel until the desired weight is achieved and then held in place by a cork.

Lead Tip Pin (Tip Weight): A short piece of lead that is epoxied into a shaft from the tip end prior to shaft installation. Tip pins are a means of swingweighting both steel and graphite-shafted clubs, but are more commonly used with graphite shafts.

Leaf-Rule: A rule, not recognized by the USGA, in which players agree that if a ball is lost in leaves, it is not treated as a lost ball (stroke and distance penalty). This "rule" is common in certain climates (and times of the year) in which trees lose their leaves and make finding balls difficult.

Lie: (1) The angle between the shaft and the ground line when the club is measured in normal playing position. (2) The position of a ball on the ground at any point on the course. A ball in the fairway will typically be considered to have a "good" lie, one in high rough grass will be labeled as a "bad" lie.

Lift: Upward force on a golf ball as it flies.

Lift and Place: A rule that allows a player to lift his ball from a fairway lie and clean it and place it back in a preferred lie. This rule normally applies to very wet or soggy courses.

Light Weight Shaft: A weight classification of shaft that falls within 3.8 – 4.25 ounces in steel or alloy shafts and within 3.2 – 3.6 ounces related to composite shafts.

Linen Belt: Used in conjunction with a belt sander, a belt made of linen fibers used to finish ferrules on woods and irons. Also known as the "ferrule turning belt."

Line Scored: On the face of an iron or wood club, the pattern of lines or grooves on the face.

Liquidmetal^{TM}: A proprietary combination of metals designed by the Liquidmetal^{TM} Golf Company. The special alloy is designed to feel soft, yet have a high coefficient of restitution.

Loading (Shaft Loading): The point of maximum energy buildup in a shaft as it is swung.

Locktite Shaft Holder: Type of shaft holder, made of aluminum or steel, used to tightly secure the club in a vise, usually for steel reshafting procedures. Not recommended for graphite shaft use.

Loft: The angle created as measured from the center of the club face in relation to the hosel bore or the angle of the club face as related to the shaft position.

Lorythmic Swingweight Scale: A type of swingweight scale that measures swingweight at a point 14" down from the butt end of the club and displays those measurements in letter/number designations (D1, D2, etc.)

Low Balance Point (LBP): A shaft that has a high percentage of its weight toward the tip. Such shafts are designed to assist in positioning more mass toward or behind the hitting area of the club. LBP shafts will tend to create clubs with higher than normal swingweights.

Low Launch: Shaft designed with a stiffer tip section to produce lower trajectory shots. Also a term used to describe golf balls designed for low initial launch trajectory due to their dimple design.

Low Profile Head: An iron or wood head that is smaller from topline to soleline than typical.

Low Riser: Slang term given to a shot, intentionally played, that starts out low and ends at a "normal" trajectory.

M

M1 Bore: The bore type in a wood in which there is 1 ½" from the ground line to the point at which the shafr bottoms out in the hosel. Also known as he "standard bore" or "metal wood bore."

M2 Bore: Type of wood bore I which the shaft bottoms out in the hosel 1" from the ground line.

Mandrel: A tapered steel rod around which composite materials are wrapped when making a shaft.

Master: The exact replica (typically made from brass or aluminum) of a wood, iron or putter head from which all heads will be duplicated.

Maxwell Hosel: Hosel design of antique wooden shafted clubs in which the hosel has holes drilled in it to reduce weight.

Medalist: The golfer with the lowest score in the qualifying round of a tournament.

Medallion: Any number of mylar and urethane type units which are affixed commonly in the cavities of woods or putters, but may also appear on metal woods. The units are designed for cosmetic urposes, enhancing the attractiveness of the club heads.

Melonite^{TM}: A plating applied to heads that is designed to prevent corrosion. The plating gives the heads a black appearance.

Metal Matrix Composite (MMC): Any of a number of alloys used to produce either a golf club or a shaft.

Metal Wood Bore: The bore configuration of a type of metal wood head in which the standard distance from the groundline to the bottom of the bores is 1 ½".

Micro Cavity: Design feature from Cleveland Golf in which weight is removed from the tpoline of the cavity of an iron. This weight is then redistributed to another location in the head.

Micro Fine Steel (MFS): Stainless steel driver face material that allows the face to achieve a very high Rockwell Hardness approaching HRC50. MFS also has comparatively high yield and tensile strengths.

Mid Launch: Type of shaft design which yields a ball flight in the "middle" trajectory range. Also a ball design term.

Midsize Wood: Any wood that approximates a 185cc size.

Milled Face: A club face, usually on a putter, that has, on a specialized machine, its face milled to .001" for flatness.

Modulus: The measure of a fiber's stiffness or resistance to bending. The higher the modulus, the stiffer the material.

Moisture Cure Polyurethane: Type of polyurethane that relies on moisture in the air for its curing properties.

Moment of Inertia (MOI): The resistance to twisting of any golf club head when that head is impacted off-center.

Momentus: A brand name for a weighted golf swing training aid popularized by PGA Tour players, among them David Duval.

Monel: An alloy of rustless metal used for club heads in the early part of the 20th century.

Mortite: Adhesive, rope-like material used to form a dam around the face insert of a wooden club prior to using pour in place insert epoxy.

Multi-Material Shaft: A shaft that is comprised of a graphite (composite) portion as well as a steel portion. Such two-piece shaft establishes unique bending properties when compared to a typical one-material shaft.

Multi-metal: Generic term given to any golf club that has two or materials in its composition. For example, a stainless steel iron with brass sole weights is considered to be a multi-metal iron.

N

Nick: Type of shaft, developed by Rapport Composite, which utilizes a filament wound longer (main body) portion and a sheet wrapped tip section to tightly control bend and flex point.

Non-Conforming Ball: Any ball that does not meet the requirements as set forth in Appendix III of the USGA Rules of Golf.

Non-Conforming Club: A club whose construction does not allow it to be played in any event (either professional, amateur or club-level) as sanctioned by USGA Rules. This includes any round of golf that will be used when establishing or maintaining a USGA handicap.

Non-Conforming Club (Driver) List: A comprehensive listing of clubs (particularly drivers) that do not meet with USGA equipment requirements for one reason or another. The list, updated regularly, is available at www. usga.org.

Nylon Deburring Wheel: Attachment (approximately 5 ½ " in diameter) to a bench grinder or similar machine that is used to remove small bits of metal from a golf club head or shaft tip.

O

OEM (Original Equipment Manufacturer): A golf club company that, as its main concern, sells complete clubs either on the wholesale level or to the general public.

Official Swingweight Scale: A type of swingweight scale that uses a 12" fulcrum as its measuring point, providing balance in ounces and total weight in ounces or grams.

Offset: The distance from the forward most point of the hosel to the leading edge of the blade. Offset will help a player who slices to align the club face with the target, thus reducing the slice. Offset may also have an effect of producing a higher ball flight.

Oil Modified Polyurethane: Type of polyurethane used by most clubmakers, it cures from the bottom layer of finish to the top. Characterized by the slight amber color, it requires no special humidity-controlled conditions.

Onset (Negative Offset): The design of a head in which the leading edge of the blade or face is forward of the leading edge of the hosel.

Overall Weight: Also known as total weight or static weight, total weight is the weight of the entire assembled club as expressed in ounces or grams. Also known as "Static Weight" or "Total Weight."

Over-Hosel: Type of shaft-to-head assembly in which the shaft fits over the post protruding from the head. Not nearly as common as the in-hosel assemblies, over-hosel applications are used on irons and putters only.

Oversized Hosel: Any wood hosel larger than .335" or any iron hosel larger than .370" is considered to be an oversized hosel.

Oversized Iron Head: The generic name given to any number of iron heads larger than standard. A standard iron has a blade height of approximately 43 millimeters and a blade length of 75 mm.

Oversized Shaft Tip: An iron shaft with a tip larger than .370" or a wood with a tip larger than .335". Certain manufacturers claim that the larger tip diameter shafts will assist in the stabilization of club heads, especially on off-center impacts.

Oversized Wood Heads: A wood having a volume between 200 and 250 cc's.

P

Parallel Tip Section: Section of the shaft toward the tip that exhibits one constant diameter up to the first step.

Parallel Tip Shaft: The type of shaft construction in which the shaft has one constant diameter in its tip section. .370" is a common tip size for parallel tip iron shafts while .335" is common for wood shafts.

Path: The imaginary line formed by the arc of a player's swing.

Pebax (Shore D Pebax): Proprietary insert material for putters developed by TaylorMade.

Perimeter Weighting: The design concept of redistributing the weight on the head to the heel and toe in an attempt to stabilize the club on all types of impacts.

Phillip Head Screw: Type of screw, as identified by its head pattern, used on certain soleplates and wooden wood face inserts.

Pixel: Individual "dot" of material utilized to comprise a club's face insert.

Playability Factor: The combination of all factors of club head design – weight, CG, head shape, etc – when determining who best fits the club head. For Example, a head that is oversized and has a low CG would have a playability factor favoring an inconsistent golfer who has trouble getting the ball airborne. Pioneered by Golfworks.

Pole: The upper and lower areas of a ball, much like the poles of a globe.

Power Fade: A shot, generally from the tee, that combines the control of a left to right fade with the power and distance of a pull.

Progressive Face Technology: Generic term applied to any club face of varying thickness.

Progressive Flexibility: A shafting concept in which longer iron have more offset and flexible shafts to promote feel and aid in getting the ball airborne and shorter irons utilize stiffer shafts for added control.

Progressive Offset: Iron head design feature in which longer iron have more offset and shorter irons have less. More offset is featured in longer irons as offset tends to eliminate slicing and helps to get the ball airborne, qualities that help most players hit the ball straighter.

Progressive Torque: A set of shafts which exhibits a changing of torque from one shaft to another through the set. Typically the torque will be greater in the longer irons and less in the shorter shafts.

Proprietary: Any feature of a golf club that is unique to a particular manufacturer.

Prorhythmic Swingweight Scale: A type of swingweight scale that bases its measurements on a 14" fulcrum system, additionally providing weights in ounces or grams.

Pour In Place Insert: Epoxy-based mixture used to replace broken or missing inserts in wooden wood.

Pry Bar: Tool used in the most economic method of graphite shaft removal.

Pured: A shaft that has been spine-aligned following the patented spinning process. A shaft that is pured will be placed in a club in its neutral position in accordance with USGA Rules.

Puring: The process of aligning a shaft so that it is in its neutral position in a club.

Q

QC: Quality Control. The process of ensuring any component of a club is with specific tolerances. The process of ensuring that a given club meets quality standards.

QPQ: Matte black finish applied to iron heads. QPQ is both a cosmetic finish and is a rust preventative as well.

R

Rails: Found on the doles of metal woods, rails function to lower the CG of the club and to provide less resistance as the club travels through the turf.

Ram Rod: Long @48") thin @3/8") rod used to force a cork down a steel shaft when using lead or tungsten powder a swingweight material.

Raw: Generic term applied to an un-plated carbon steel iron or wedge head. Raw heads are most common related to wedges; the head will rust over time.

Reamer: Type of drill bit used to enlarge a hosel to one uniform parallel tip diameter.

Reed and Prince Screw: Type of screw, as identified by its head pattern, used on certain soleplates and wooden wood face inserts.

Refinish: The process of applying a completely new finish to a wooden or metal head. The refinish involves removing the old finish prior to applying the new finish.

Relative Stiffness: The stiffness of a shaft when compared to another shaft or shafts.

Regrip: The process of installing a new grip onto a club.

Reset Insert, Soleplate or Backweight, ect.: The process of removing and re-epoxying (and perhaps re-installing screws) any loose part of the head as indicated.

Reshaft: The process of installing a new shaft into a club head.

Ribbed Grip: A grip that has a raised section along the length of the back of the grip. Certain players believe a ribbed grip will help them maintain uniform hand position on all clubs in the set.

Rider: Slang term, usually applied to a beginner's shot, in which that shot has been hit far enough that the player has to ride in a cart (rather than walk) to hit the next shot. Somewhat of a derogatory term applied to the skill of a beginner.

Rifle™ Shaft: Manufactured by Royal Precision Golf, the Rifle™ shaft is a steel shaft that is characterized by its lack of steps. Brunswick claims the shaft combines the consistency of steel with the dampening properties of graphite.

Rocker Sole: Also known as Camber. The radius measurement of the sole of a club. A sole can be cambered (a slightly arched surface) from toe to heel, or from front to back, or both.

Rolled: term given to a shot that does not get airborne and simply rolls along the ground.

Roll Face™ **Putter**: Patented by Teardrop™ Golf, Roll Face™ putters feature a uniformly curving face from top to sole.

Rouge: Compound used in conjunction with stitched buffing wheel to polish marks from stainless steel heads.

Round Grip: A grip that tapers uniformly the entire distance along its length and has no discernible ribs.

RSSR (Recommended Swing Speed Rating): Shaft fitting system developed by Golfsmith International as a guide to identify a shaft well-suited to a player's swing.

Rubber-Core Ball: Introduced in 1898, the rubber core ball consisted of a solid rubber center around which was wound elastic thread under tension. The cover was made from gutta-percha. This ball, also called the Haskell, as it was invented by Colburn Haskell, is considered to have revolutionized the game.

Rusty: Generic term applied to an un-plated carbon steel iron or wedge head. Rusty heads are most common related to wedges; the head will rust over time.

S

Sandblast: Finish applied to the faces and cavities of certain irons. Metal wood heads may also have sandblasted finishes. Characterized by a light gray color, these finishes are applied through the use of an air compressor and special sandblast gun. The common media used for sandblasting is aluminum oxide sand.

Sandblasting Cabinet: Box-like cabinet with a window and arm-holes used for sandblasting golf clubs.

Sanding Belts: Long thin belts of various grits used in conjunction with belt sanders in golf club repair shops.

Sanding Cone: Attachment for a motor or specialized sanding station. Cone or cylindrical (drum) shaped and covered with sandpaper held in place by two-way tape.

Satin Finish: Type of finish applied to stainless steel iron heads and metal wood soles through a series of finishing belts.

Scared Neck: Wooden shafted club construction in which the shaft and head are joined by glue and whipping. Also called a "Splice Neck."

Scotchbrite Wheel: Type of wheel mounted on a bench grinder used to return a club's finish to satin. Also known as "Surebrite Wheel."

Scriber: Tool with wooden or plastic handle and sharp metallic point used to clean out screw holes, engravings, etc.

Segmented Flex Technology: From Aldila, the concept of producing a shaft with a tip section significantly smaller that the body of the shaft. The technology is used to control launch angles in the various designs of shafts.

Sensicore™: A vibration dampening core, developed by True Temper™, and inserted into the shaft to reduce vibration. Sensicores are used in both wood and iron shafts, steel and graphite.

Sensicore Gold: A line of shafts from True Temper in which the size of the Sensicore shaft insert varies through the set. The Sensicores are larger in the longer irons and shorter in the wedges in a set of Sensicore Gold shafts.

Shaft Cutting Board: Wooden or metal board, usually attached to a chop saw that measures and cuts a number of shafts at one time.

Shaft Extension: A piece of material inserted into the butt of the shaft to make it longer.

Shaft Identification (ID) Gauge: Retangular aluminum gauge used to measure shaft tip size, step patterns and helpful in identifying shaft types.

Shaft Lab: Computerized system of shaft fitting developed by True Temper that places a high emphasis on how a player "loads" a shaft during the swing. Shaft lab provides computer readouts and graphics as part of its fitting system.

Shaft Lag: Situation in which the club head lags behind the shaft toward impact as a result of the natural flexion of the shaft.

Shaft Puller: Specialized tool used in the removal of graphite shafts from steel or titanium club heads.

Shafting Beads: Small nylon (or other non-abrasive material) beads, when mixed with epoxy, that helps center a shaft in the Hosel.

Shallow Face: Any wood or iron having a face height less than the norm. Shallow face clubs typically have lower CG's, thus making it easier to get the ball airborne.

Shanked Ferrule: Ferrule, with a raised lip at its top, used in conjunction with wooden woods. The "shank" or lip, helps clubmakers begin the whipping without slippage.

Shear Strength: Resistance of material (i.e. epoxy) to being broken or torn apart.

Sheet Wrapping: The process of making a graphite shaft in which sheets of graphite and epoxy resin are wrapped around a mandrel to produce a shaft. Also known as "Table Rolling."

Shim: This metallic sleeve, paper wedge or metal spring used to center a shaft in a hosel or to fit smaller tipped sgafts into larger bore hosels.

Short-Shafting: The process of installing a shaft short of the bottom of the hosel bore. In effect this makes the shaft play softer than it was designed to play. Most common in deep bore metal heads.

Shot Peen Finish: Type of finish applied to stainless steel iron heads that leaves the appearance of a "silvery, semi-rough" surface.

Silkscreen: A method of identification found on most shafts. On steel shafts, it typically encircles the shaft approximately ¼ of the distance from the shaft tip, and is usually black in color. On raphite shafts, it is typically located near the grip and is much more colorful and noticeable.

Skving: The thin edges on the underside or a leather or other wrap-on grip, making the grip easier to wrap in place.

Slope (Index): Mathematical formula used to compare the difficulty of one course to the next. It takes into account length, hazards, terrain, etc. A course with a slope rating of 150 will be far more difficult than one sloped at 100. Slope ratings allow fair mathes between members from clubs of varying difficulty.

Snake: A long putt; one that is usually holed from a long distance.

Sod: A chunk of turf from the course, called a divot.

Soft Spikes: Generic term given to the plastic type of spikes required on many courses. The softer spikes are believed to do less damage to the course, especially to the greens.

Soft-Stepping: A process of assembly in which a shaft with longer tip section is put into a club that would normally require a shorter tip section in order that the club play to a softer flex.

Softie: General term given to a one-piece grip composed of a very soft compound. First developed by the Eaton Corporation and marketed under the Golf Pride name.

Sole Weight Iron: The design of an iron head in which the majority of its weight is concentrated toward the sole of the club. This produces a lower CG.

Sole Width: The measure of a sole from the leading edge to the trailing edge. A narrow sole width is better from firmer ground; wide soles are helpful in getting the ball airborne and are more suited to less-firm ground.

SP700: A type of beta titanium face used on high-end titanium driver. SP700 allows the face to be made stronger and thinner, potentially increasing its COR.

Specification (Specs) Gauge: A specialized piece of equipment used to measure a club's loft. Lie, face angle, offset and face progression.

Spikes: Metal implements on the bottom of golf shoes designed to aid in traction. Spikes are approximately ½" in length. "Spikes" may also be a slang term used for golf shoes themselves.

Spine Alignment: Process of locating a shaft's spine and positioning it either toward or away from the target in a club in accordance with USGA Rules. Also called "spinning."

Spinner Shaft: Rifle-Type wedge shaft made by Royal Precision that is softer than a typical wedge shaft. This allows more feel and control on wedge shots.

Spine: The point of a shaft in which it exhibits uniform bending properties in relation to the target.

Spring Face: Generic term applied to any titanium driver or drive face, particularly to those whose face in made from a specialized alloy such as SP700, 15-3-3-3, etc.

Spring-Like Effect: A general term given to the faces of metal woods related to how much the face compresses and decompresses (springs back) upon ball impact. The USGA recently established standards for this effect, based upon their assumption that is a face springs more, overall ball distance may be increased, making some of today's courses obsolete. Also called the "Trampoline Effect."

Square (Box, "U") Grooves: Face lines (or grooves) pressed, cut or cast into a rectangular shape during manufacturing.

Standard Size Wood: Any wood head that approximates a volume of 150cc.

Standard Weight Shaft: A steel shaft weight classification that falls within the range of 4.25-4.62 ounces.

Stableford: Type of competition in which points are awarded in relation to a fixed score on each hole. For example, a par may receive 0 points, a birdie, 2 points, and eagle 5 points, double eagle 8 points, and a bogie -1 point.

Static Fitting: The process of fitting an individual without actually watching him or her hit balls.

Step: Location on a steel shaft where the diameter of the shaft steps up" noticeably to a larger diameter. The average steel shaft has numerous steps arranged in a pattern unique to that shaft's specific model allowing clubmakers to distinguish one unmarked shaft from another.

Stepless: Term describing a steel shaft that contains no "steps up" in diameter, making instead the transition from thin to thicker in a smooth, gradual manner. FCM Rifle and Apollo Balistik are stepless shafts.

Step Drilling: A method of enlarging the bore of a hosel through the use of a series of drill bits. The process is begun with the smallest drill bit, then progresses to a medium sized bit, followed by a larger sized bit. Step drilling makes the process of enlarging a hosel bore easier and less time-consuming.

Stitching Buffing Wheel: Type of wheel used , along with a bench grinder and Emery Cake, Tripoli or Rouge compounds, to polish stainless steel heads.

Strong Loft: The loft of any club, particularly an iron, that is less than the standard specifications for that club. Strong lofted clubs tend to hit the ball lower and longer than standard lofts, but may sacrifice some control.

Stronomic™: Proprietary face insert material from Odyssey™ Golf that helped to first popularize face insert putter designs.

Studio Design: Trademark name given to a line of milled putters made by Scotty Cameron for Titleist.

Subflex: In the True temper stiff Dynamic Gold series, for example, each individual flex S200, S300, S400 are all subflexes of stiff.

Supination: A term made porpular by Ben Hogan referring to the rotation and angling of the right wrist during the golf swing.

Super-Steel: Any number of alloys of steel that are stronger and often lighter than the 17-4 type of steel used commonly in metal woods.

Surlyn™: A thermoplastic resin cover, invented by DuPont in the late 1970's, Surlyn™ is a very common material in durable cover balls.

Swaging: A method of shaft manufacture, in which the tip of the shaft is elongated in order to make it a specific smaller diameter.

Sweet Swing: Term given to a player who swings at the ball in a skilled manner.

Swing Computer: Device used in club fitting to accurately define swing characteristics such as swing path, swing speed, tempo, face angle, etc. Also called the "swing analyzer."

Swingweight Scale: A measuring scale specific to golf clubs that utilize a balance system to determine the swingweight and possibly the total weight of a golf club.

T

Taper Tip Shaft: One of a number of shafts manufactured with a tip section that varies in length and thickness below the first step. This type of shaft requires that a specific length, known as a discreet length, shaft be made for each club in a set. Taper tip shafts are more commonly used by OEM's as compared to custom clubmakers.

Tempo Trainer: Computerized device, sometimes used in fitting, that determines the pace of a player's swing. This information is then transferred by the fitter into a shaft/head recommendations for the player.

Tensil Strength: Resistance of a material to being stretched or elongated.

Teryllium™: Proprietary insert material used by Titleist™ in many of their Scotty Cameron putters. The material is a mix of many alloys producing a softer feeling insert for putters.

Thermoplastic: A type of shaft material that once formed may be re-shaped or re-formed. The Phoenixx TPC company, formerly Quadrax™, experienced limited success with this type of shaft.

Thermoplastic Hosel: The hosel of a golf club produced from some type of thermoplastic material. Allowing it to be constructed to produce specific lie and face angles. Ping developed this type of hosel for proprietary used in its titanium drivers.

Thermoset: An epoxy based material that, once formed, cannot be re-shaped or re-formed.

Through-Bore (Thru-Bore) Plug: Plastic, wooden or graphite plug inserted into the shaft tip in through-bore shaft applications to cosmetically finish the shaft tip.

Ti-Alloy: A metallic alloy used for wood heads that contains some titanium. Typically ti-alloy heads are comprised mostly of aluminum and are considered to be of lesser quality than other head materials.

Tip Diameter: The outside diameter of a shaft tip as measured at the very tip of the shaft. Also called "Tip Size."

Tip Flexible: A shaft whose tip is specifically designed to be softer than the body of the shaft. Tip flexible yields high trajectories for most golfers.

Tip Heavy: A shaft whose tip section is generally heavier than a similar length section of the shaft butt.

Tip Pin: A short piece of lead that is inserted into the shaft from the tip end prior to shaft installation. Tip pins are a means of swingweighting both steel and graphite-shafted clubs, but are more commonly used with graphite shafts. Also known as "Tip Weight."

Tip Stiff: A shaft whose tip is measurably stiff as compared to other sections of the shaft. Used by harder swinging players.

Tip to First Step: Measurement used by certain companies to assist in shaft trimming prior to shaft installation.

Tip Trim: The process of cutting a shaft from the tip end prior to shaft installation. Also known as "Tipping" or "Tip Trimming" and is used to increase the stiffness of the shaft.

Toe Weighted: Design concept of placing a high concentration of weight toward the toe of a club.

Topdress: Fertilizer, soil and sand mix applied to greens after they are aerified in order to provide nutrients to the green.

Topline: The uppermost part of an iron blade, running from heel to toe.

Torque: The resistance of a shaft to twisting is its torque. Lower torque shafts twist less and may be recommended for stronger players. Torque is also used to define the relationship between the turning of the upper and lower body during the swing.

Tour Weighted: The somewhat generic term applied to composite shafts that weight approximately the dame as standard weight steel shafts @ 125 grams.

Track: The layout of a golf course. Also the term given to a putt as it roll toward the hole.

Trajectory: The shape and height of a shot in relation to its direction.

Trailing Edge: The most rearward part of a club's sole.

Tri-Metal: A club head comprised of three separate materials. Popularized by Orlimar™, a tri-metal type head may contain 17-4 stainless steel body, maraging steel face and a copper alloy in sole rails.

Trim Ring: Small plastic ring found at the top of certain ferrules. Trim rings, decorative in nature, may be any number of colors. Most clubmakers do not use trim rings a great deal due to a lack of durability over time.

Tripoli: Compound used in conjunction with a stitched buffing wheel to polish marks from a stainless head.

Trouble Club: A category of clubs that is utilized to extricate the ball from a difficult lie. Trouble clubs often have a unique sole construction- perhaps rails – that lowers the CG of the clubs, making them easy to hit from less desirable positions on the course. The club may be an iron, a wood or a hybrid club.

True Measure: Club length measuring device, generally placed on a bench, that takes into account the lie of a club when measuring its length. A very accurate way to measure club length.

Tubing (Shaft) Cutter: Hand operated tool used to cut steel shaft tips and butts. Using the tool is very labor-intensive; it is used strictly for small-volume shops.

Tumble Finish: Type of finish applied to iron and metal wood heads via a specialized tumbling machine, called the Tumbler, containing various tumbling media. Finish is characterized by its dull durable look.

Tuned Weight Cartridge: Developed by TaylorMade for use in the 500 series titanium drivers, a weighting system that is claimed to position the CG of the club to match a given player. Visible by looking at the back of the driver head.

Tungsten: A heavy metallic compound used to add weight to a club head, either as a swingweight material in the shaft or as a defined weight attached somewhere in/on the head.

TX-90: Developed by True Temper, a specialized steel alloy allowing steel shafts to be made under the 100-gram weight range.

U

U-Groove: Type of groove used in iron face structure. More pronounced than traditional "V" grooves.

Ultralight Shaft: A class of composite shafts that weigh less than 2 ounces or 65 grams.

Undercut Cavity: Also known as "Channel Back", a club design in which a channel or cavity is created through the addition of weight along the back cavity of a club.

Underlisting: The rubber or paper material onto which a leather grip is wrapped.

Unitized: A shaft in which one model can be used to build one entire set of irons or a one model may be used to build a full set of woods through successive trimming of the shaft tip section.

Unloading (Shaft Unloading): The point of maximum energy release as a shaft is swung.

Un-plated: A club made from carbon steel that has not been plated.

Unstitched Buffing Wheel: Type of wheel used along with a bench grinder and Glanz Wach to add a high luster to polyurethane-coated club heads.

Urethane: A synthetic cover material of a golf ball that is durable, yet that produces a soft feel. Urethane cover balls are typically among the more expensive balls on the market, but are gaining popularity among professional golfers due to their playability.

V

Variable Face: A golf club face that exhibits a different face thickness on one or more area of the face. Typically, variable face irons have thicker faces toward the sole, while variable face woods usually have a thinner face perimeters and thicker centers. The process of construction is called "Variable Face Technology."

Very Lightweight Shaft: A weight classification of shafts that falls within 3.40-3.79 ounces weight range for steel or alloy shafts and 2-3.19 ounces for composite shafts.

Velocity: The speed of a golf ball. Also known as initial velocity, the USGA limits conforming balls to velocities of no more than 250 feet per second (76.2m/s) as measured on USGA test equipment. A 2% tolerance is allowed at a test temperature of 23 degrees Celsius +/-1.

Vertical Flow Weighting: The method of flow weighting in which the weight moves vertically from concentration of weight toward the sole of long irons to more traditional weighting on short irons.

Vinyl Shaft Clamp: Type of clamp used to hold a club in a vise. Also called "Vice Pads."

Viscoelastic Material: A proprietary material used by the leveland Golf Company to assist in providing vibration absorption in their patented VAS™ clubs.

Volume: A numerical designation given to the size of a wood head as measured by liquid displacement.

W

Waste Area: An area on a golf course that is similar to a sand trap, but is not declared an official hazard. It is generally not maintained or raked and is often comprised of shells, pebbles or very course sand.

Water Hazard: Any relatively permanent and open area of water (sea, lake, pond, etc.) anywhere on the course. The penalty for hitting your ball into a water hazard, that you cannot hit out of, is one stroke.

Weight Sorted: Club components that are weighed prior to assembly in an attempt to ensure consistent specification of the finished club.

Whins: A British term for extremely heavy areas of rough.

Whipping Cover: Plastic cover installed over the string whipping on certain woods.

Whisper: Soft two-piece type of grip produced by Golf Pride in response to the popularity of softer grips.

Windings: The elastic rubber material tightly wrapped around the core of some three-piece balls. Typically 35 yards of material will be stretched to over 250 yards in a single ball.

Winn-Type Grip: A type of grip that is generally considered to be softer than typical. Winn produced the first of today's popular soft grip designs, but also does manufacture grips of varying firmness and material.

Wry Neck: Scottish name for an offset or gooseneck putter.

X

"X" Factor: Applies to the differential between hip angle and shoulder angle during golfer's backswing.

X-out: General term given to less than perfect balls. Usually top grade balls with a slight cosmetic or manufacturing defect, WX-outs are identified by a row of "X's" or the words "X-OUT" somewhere on the cover.

Y

Yardage Marker: An object that indicates how far a specific location is from the middle of the green. Common yardage markers are often found at 250, 200, 150, 100 and 50 yards from the green. 150 yard makers can be painted markers in the fairway, white or black and white posts on both sides of the fairway, sometimes as a single post in the middle of the fairway, or trees or bushes along the side of the fairway.

Z

Zinc Iron Heads: Iron heads die cast from an alloy of zinc usually found as beginner clubs.

Zirconium: Element used as a face coating or material for wedges, adding to increase the apin due to the surface roughness provided by the zirconium.

Zylin: A proprietary cover material developed by Spalding that is claimed to produce feel and durability.

References

All glossary terms were taken from the internet at: www.swingweight.com and www.golfinsite.net .

Rockwell Hardness Scale
The Industry Reference Standard
By Jeff Jackson, Mitchell Golf
From the internet at www.swingweight.com

Material	Hardness	Primary Use
Aluminum	B50 – 60	Woods, Putters Softest
Carbon Steel	B60 – 70	Irons, Putters
304 Stainless	B75	Irons Only
Beryllium Copper	B70 – 80	Irons, Putters
431 Stainless	18 – 25	Irons, Putters
100% Titanium	C24 – 28	Woods
6 – 4 Titanium	C32 – 36	Woods, Faces
17 – 4 Stainless	C34 – 38	Woods, irons, Putters
450 Steel	C36 – 40	Woods, Irons (supersteel)
15 – 5 Stainless	C36 – 44	Woods
Beta Titanium	C40+	Woods
Maraging Steel	C45 – 55	Woods, faces Hardest

Other alloys are listed below that did not appear on the list above and has no Rockwell Hardness scale number:

Bronze	Nickel Stainless	Titan-Steel
15-3-3-3 Stainless		1030 Carbon Steel
304 Stainless Steel		Nickel Cobalt
18-8 Stainless	Marafing Steel	